THE IMPOSSIBLE INDIAN

FAISAL DEVJI

THE IMPOSSIBLE INDIAN

Gandhi and the Temptation of Violence

Harvard University Press
Cambridge, Massachusetts
2012

Copyright © Faisal Devji, 2012
All rights reserved
Printed in the United States of America

First published in the United Kingdom in 2012 by
C. Hurst & Co. (Publishers) Ltd.,
41 Great Russell Street,
London, WC1B 3PL

First Harvard University Press edition, 2012

Library of Congress Cataloging-in-Publication Data

Devji, Faisal.
The impossible Indian : Gandhi and the temptation of violence / Faisal Devji.
p. cm.
Includes bibliographical references and index.
ISBN 978-0-674-06672-4 (cloth : alk. paper)
1. Gandhi, Mahatma, 1869–1948—Philosophy. 2. Gandhi, Mahatma, 1869–1948—Political and social views. 3. India—History—Sepoy Rebellion, 1857–1858—Influence. 4. Statesmen—India—Biography.
I. Title.
DS481.G3D4465   2012
954.03'5092—dc23   [B]   2012019637

CONTENTS

Acknowledgements   vii

Introduction   1

1. Bastard History   9
2. A Nation Misplaced   41
3. In Praise of Prejudice   67
4. Brothers in Arms   93
5. Hitler's Conversion   119
6. Leaving India to Anarchy   151

Conclusion   185

Notes   193
Index   207

ACKNOWLEDGEMENTS

An admirer of Gandhi's, my father kept a framed photograph of the Mahatma in his Dar-es-Salaam office. But though I grew up with a sense of respect for the old man depicted seated at his spinning wheel in this image, it was only when I'd finished my formal education that I felt the seductive force of his ideas. Much of my work since then has been informed by a fascination with Gandhi's thought, even though very little of it has dealt explicitly with the Mahatma. This book is an attempt to render visible my obligation to Gandhi's ideas, while at the same time making what I hope is a new case for their author to be considered one of the great political thinkers of our times.

I owe many and varied thanks to friends and colleagues over a lengthy period, whose insights into Gandhi's career have informed my writing of this book. Foremost among them is Uday Mehta, with whom I've been talking about the Mahatma during our peregrinations across three continents. In New Haven and then New York, conversations with Carol Breckenridge and Arjun Appadurai, as well as Vyjayanthi Rao and Satya Pemmaraju, contributed much to my understanding of the Mahatma's international career and ambiguous heritage in modern India. The course on violence and nonviolence that Vyjayanthi and I taught at The New School For Social Research in 2008 allowed me to gather my thoughts on Gandhi's politics, as did the conferences that Ritu Birla and I organized in Johannesburg in 2009 and Mumbai in

ACKNOWLEDGEMENTS

2010 on the Mahatma's first book, *Hind Swaraj*, and the special issue of *Public Culture* that we edited from the papers presented there. I'm also grateful for the conversations I had with Akeel Bilgrami and Ajay Skaria during this period.

More recently, between New York and Oxford, I have benefitted enormously from discussions with Richard Sorabji, Chris Bayly and in particular Shruti Kapila, with whom I edited a set of essays on Indian political thought for *Modern Intellectual History* in 2010. Shruti has been the single most important force preventing my wholesale seduction by all things Gandhian. I am also grateful to David Arnold, Dipesh Chakrabarty and Ruth Harris for their advice on the drafts and portions of my manuscript they so generously read. My colleagues at the South Asia History Seminar in Oxford provided me with the scholarly context in which this book was conceived, for which I want to thank Polly O'Hanlon, Aparna Kapadia, Sarmila Bose, Maria Misra and Judith Brown, whose two volumes on Gandhi remain the authoritative account of his career. I also want to thank Agnibho Gangopadhyay for checking and correcting my Gandhi citations at the Bodleian. To Rachel and Michael Dwyer I owe a great debt for their intellectual as well as more material hospitality, and to Christophe Carvalho my thanks for affording me the leisure to write in Mumbai and Goa.

Portions of this book have appeared previously in the following journals, whose publishers I would like to thank for permission to reprint these texts:

"A Practice of Prejudice: Gandhi's Politics of Friendship", *Subaltern Studies X11*, 2005. Reprinted with permission by Permanent Black.

"The Mutiny to Come", *New Literary History*, vol. 40, no. 2, Spring 2009, pp. 411–430. Adapted with permission by The Johns Hopkins University Press.

"Morality in the Shadow of Politics", *Modern Intellectual History*, vol. 7, no. 2, July 2010, pp. 373–390. Reproduced with the permission of Cambridge University Press.

ACKNOWLEDGEMENTS

"The Paradox of Nonviolence", *Public Culture*, vol. 23, no. 2, Spring 2011, pp. 269–274. Reprinted by permission of the publisher, Duke University Press.

Faisal Devji   Oxford, March 2012

INTRODUCTION

Towards the end of his memoir describing the events leading up to India's independence in 1947, the labor activist Kanji Dwarkadas summed up the character of Gandhi, whom he had known for nearly thirty years, in the following irate paragraph:

> Gandhiji appealed to the imagination of the world as a little, scrawny, half-starved, self-denying man in a breach-clout—a wizened little monkey defying the terrible British lion—a sort of incarnation of Hanuman, the monkey-god, as I heard one intellectual, non-Congress Indian describe him. This Gandhi has been apotheosized by the millions of the Indian masses today. His very irrationality, his mystical defiance of the principles of common sense, his persistence in spite of his "Himalayan blunders", the frequent success of his fantastic, almost crack-brained schemes, endeared him to both the masses and the extremist intellectuals.[1]

Uncharitable though it may be, this description of the Mahatma from a book with a foreword written by Clement Attlee, who as Britain's prime minister had presided over the dissolution of her Indian empire, nicely represents the bafflement of Gandhi's friends as well as enemies when faced with his politics of nonviolence. Leaving aside figures who, like Churchill, were altogether opposed to India's independence, even those who desired and fought for her freedom were often frustrated by the Mahatma's politics, which accorded with the aims neither of his partisans on the left nor indeed on the right. And Dwarkadas is as scornful of these figures, like the Congress leaders Jawaharlal

Nehru and Vallabhbhai Patel, who he thought had gained power by latching onto Gandhi while mostly disagreeing with his politics, as he is of those Hindu or Muslim nationalists who opposed the Mahatma from outside the Indian National Congress, each by accusing him of betraying their community to the other.

Dwarkadas acknowledged Gandhi's moral sincerity as well as his tremendous popular appeal, but was appalled at the toll in life, suffering and internal conflict that he thought the politics of nonviolence had taken in India over three decades. And so the historical narrative he offers in this book and others that he wrote is one in which the Mahatma's practices of non-cooperation or civil disobedience are seen as interrupting and delaying a constitutional process leading to the country's independence, which was eventually achieved only at the cost of a partition between its Hindu and Muslim territories accompanied by immense massacres, migrations and a never-ending confrontation with Pakistan, the unwanted new partner in India's freedom.

As a liberal suspicious of Gandhi's politics, Dwarkadas emphasizes what he sees as its futility, and in doing so voices the one argument that unites all of the Mahatma's critics, who think his career a failure because it manifested either too much or too little of a virtue like nonviolence. Details apart, such arguments represent a basic judgment, namely that Gandhi was a politician unable to achieve his objective, a single independent country at peace with itself and its neighbors. Whether or not the counterfactual narrative Dwarkadas then presents of history without the Mahatma is persuasive, envisioning as it does an undivided India gaining the status of a self-governing dominion like Canada before the Second World War, and with Pakistan's founder Mohammad Ali Jinnah as her first prime minister, what is revealing is its dawning recognition that Gandhi's nonviolent politics might not simply have been about independence after all.

The Mahatma had always claimed that India's independence was pointless if all it meant was replacing white faces with

INTRODUCTION

brown ones, or merely gaining for Indians the political freedoms that Englishmen possessed. He was interested rather in an unprecedented moral transformation, seeing in nonviolence a practice that brooked no limits and had universal application, with the movement for India's freedom providing only a site in which it might be tried out as an experiment. He thought India's size and importance would guarantee the worldwide dissemination of nonviolence if its practice were to succeed there, and in doing so transform the nature of politics itself. India's mission, therefore, was not simply to liberate herself from imperialism, but set the precedent that would free the world as a whole from violence. In this sense Gandhi's politics goes well beyond nationalism, but it also has little to do with some ideal of a moral life that can be sequestered from the violent history of the twentieth century. Instead nonviolence belongs with the great revolutionary movements of its time, as Dwarkadas suggests when he notes that its gigantic mobilizations brought "extremist intellectuals" together with the "masses" in a politics that could only be seen as irrational from the viewpoint of one dedicated only to a country's independence.

It has become commonplace for historians to ascribe much of what Dwarkadas calls the Mahatma's "fantastic, almost crackbrained schemes", involving such moralistic and apparently self-destructive acts as the suspension of successful agitations against the British or the resignation of elected office, to attempts at reining in the radical drift of popular politics on the one hand and ill-advised brinkmanship to achieve more concessions from Britain on the other. Whatever the truth of these explanations, omitted from them is any consideration of the violence and suffering entailed in all of Gandhi's politics. Rather than seeing in these facts only the failure of nonviolence, however, Dwarkadas is concerned with how their occurrence never deterred the Mahatma from embarking upon actions that he knew would result in more death and destruction. For if Gandhi was horrified by the violence exercised from time to time by his followers, he longed to provoke it from those who had to be opposed by their nonviolence. It was this desire for violence that disturbed Dwarkadas, who saw it as being unnecessary in straightforward political terms, remarking that "Gandhi believes in suffering and he is not happy if he achieves his object through normal evolutionary methods. He wants to build character through suffering".[2] And indeed Gandhi was not averse to comparing the courage of revolutionary violence favorably with what he thought was the inadequate form that nonviolent suffering took in India. For he recognized the similarity between these apparently divergent courses of action, both of which resulted, after all, in the courting of arrest, punishment and even death. As he put it in 1946 to some companions in Bengal:

Bengal had tried the method of violence for a long while. The bravery of the revolutionaries was beyond question, but it had failed to instill courage in the mind of the common man. But although the non-violence of the past twenty-five years had been of an indifferent quality, yet nobody could deny that it had succeeded in elevating the character of the whole nation to a certain extent.[3]

The Mahatma's movement of nonviolent resistance, with its mass following and universal claims, its toleration of violence and the explicit desire for suffering, must surely be placed alongside the great revolutionary movements of his time. For in many ways Gandhi belongs in the same group as his contemporaries, Lenin, Hitler and Mao, and should not be seen as a moralist detached from the mainstream of twentieth-century politics. Such an appreciation of his nonviolence allows us only to ignore Gandhi as a figure central to modern history. Yet unlike the last century's impresarios of mass politics, the Mahatma did not simply tolerate violence as a means towards some end but famously prized the suffering it produced in its own right. And this made Gandhi's dealings with violence far more radical than those of his revolutionary peers, responsible though they might have

INTRODUCTION

been for much more of it than the old man in a breach-clout. Nonviolence could only prove its claim to moral superiority by being tested against violence, without any reference to a political end being required for this. And conceived of in this fundamental way, as a potential inherent in every kind of interaction, personal as much as political, nonviolence brought to light the moral dimension in all action, something obscured by the "scientific" logic of communist and fascist ideologies. Indeed the only part of science that Gandhi claimed for himself was the experiment, which is to say nothing but its method and therefore its essence. And as a method, of course, nonviolence cut across the rival systems represented by the revolutionary ideologies of Gandhi's day, refusing to propose any alternative one but making itself at home in each precisely by a series of experiments.

Nonviolence, Gandhi thought, was not only appropriate in any historical context, but also capable of giving rise to a moral order that might take any political form. It was the experiment itself that had value, with nonviolence guaranteeing the virtue of any order in which it had been accepted as a norm. But if nonviolence could make itself at home anywhere, then it could not be conceived of in historical terms. And so when the Mahatma claimed that human flourishing was due to nonviolence rather than to the force or fear of any law, he thought of this virtue as being so ubiquitous and fundamental to social relations as to possess no history of its own. Only violence, in other words, was historical, because it was sporadic and therefore transformative in the limited way that allowed historians to define it as either a cause or an effect. To bring about the reign of nonviolence in a place like India might therefore be unprecedented, but it only represented the formal recognition of a force that already sustained society. In this sense Gandhi's nonviolent revolution was a fundamentally conservative one, since he remained uninterested in beginnings or endings, and was happy for all manner of institutions and practices to exist as long as they abjured violence. Indeed he may well be described as the only mass leader of the twentieth century who not only disdained history, but also neglected the ideology that made of it an argument for the achievement of some utopia.

Unlike his revolutionary peers, for whom violence was an instrument to achieve a historical transformation that we might call utopian, Gandhi could tolerate violence and value suffering only because they offered opportunities for the display of nonviolent resistance, which he thought constituted moral as well as political sovereignty in its own right. Indeed he frequently described such resistance as the "sovereign method" or "sovereign remedy" for every kind of political ill. And if we define as sovereign any authority that can ask people to kill and die in its name, then we must recognize that what Gandhi did was to split the concept of sovereignty down the middle. By separating dying from killing and prizing the former as a nobler deed, he was doing nothing more than retrieving sovereignty from the state and generalizing it as a quality vested in individuals. For while such individuals might be unequal in their ability to kill they were all equally capable of dying, demonstrating therefore the universality of suffering and sacrifice over violence of all kinds. And because he had fragmented sovereignty in this way, Gandhi held that the nonviolent hero's most intimate rival could only be another non-state actor, the revolutionary terrorist willing to kill and die for India's freedom. Sovereign about the terrorist's act, after all, was the fact that it already represented freedom and did not serve merely as an instrument for its realization in some undefined future. Indeed the Mahatma believed that the sovereignty of terrorism resided in its sacrificial immediacy, which was what gave it nobility in the eyes of other Indians, and not in the murderous element that merely obscured it with the rhetoric of instrumentality. So in a speech made in 1916, Gandhi blamed the militants of his time for degrading the truly sovereign act of dying by killing to achieve it:

INTRODUCTION

I honor the anarchist for his love of the country. I honor him for his bravery in being willing to die for his country; but I ask him: Is killing honorable? Is the dagger of an assassin a fit precursor of an honorable death?[4]

Kanji Dwarkadas was therefore right to echo the opinion of many others and call the Mahatma a philosophical anarchist, since he not only disconnected sovereignty from the state, but also believed that the willingness to suffer and die lay in the grasp of anyone who wanted it. As early as *Hind Swaraj* or *Indian Self Rule*, his manifesto of 1909 that not coincidentally was structured as a dialogue with a revolutionary, Gandhi had contended that freedom and thus sovereignty were immediately available to anyone fearless enough to accept suffering and death by withdrawing cooperation from an unjust order. Indeed only that freedom was real which possessed this existential and therefore individual character, even if the rest of India remained in chains.[5] Eschewing the long-awaited collective utopias of revolutionary politics elsewhere, Gandhi linked his movement to the kind of immediate gratification that arguably inspires all mass action at some level. And it was because the irreducible sovereignty of this gratification seemed to be linked only accidentally to the achievement of freedom in an institutional sense that Dwarkadas suspects it. For his distrust is directed at the revolutionary aspect of nonviolence, which seemed to break with what he took to be the consequence-driven rationality of human behavior and transform it completely. But it is precisely this aspect of Gandhi's movement that interests me, one whose politics consisted of tempting violence in order to convert it by the force of suffering into something quite unexpected. So I shall not again refer to Kanji Dwarkadas or say anything more about his views.

Gandhi himself had always been clear about the fact that his movement had nothing to do with avoiding violence, but was meant rather to invite and in so doing to convert it. For it was evident to him that unlike nonviolence, which possessed only a negative meaning, violence enjoyed a positive existence and was implied in all action, including the everyday processes of living that wore down the body and eventually destroyed it. Nonviolence, therefore, was meant not to provide some alternative to violence but instead to appropriate and, as the Mahatma himself often said, to sublimate it. Hence this book focuses on Gandhi's efforts to sublimate violence by inviting and directing it through a series of political experiments, both theoretical and practical, that cannot be confined to nationalism in any conventional sense. These include a quixotic attempt to defend the British Empire against itself, laying claim to the leadership of a pan-Islamic agitation for the restoration of the Caliphate, advice to Germany's victims and especially the Jews on how to deal with Nazism in a nonviolent way, and his desire that Britain leave India to anarchy and civil war. In the following pages I shall examine the implications of these curious experiments with violence, which have received little if any attention from historians, and ask what they tell us about the limits and possibilities of nonviolence in our own time. Given his experimental approach to politics, Gandhi's various engagements with violence did not necessarily follow the same pattern, and at times even contradicted one another. They were, however, united by a set of principles whose political significance I mean to explore.

1

BASTARD HISTORY

It has become a convention for all those who write on Gandhi to spend some time tracing his intellectual and political antecedents. And these have themselves become so conventional as to be rattled off for the most part without further analysis. Thus we are told that in his childhood the future Mahatma was deeply influenced by his mother's piety, and during his time as a student of the law in London, by a sundry assortment of pacifists, vegetarians and nonconformist Christians. All of this is true enough, and Gandhi himself did not hesitate to attribute each and every one of his practices to a range of moral authorities including such well-known figures as Thoreau, Ruskin and Tolstoy. Noteworthy about this frequently recited list of names is that there are so few Indians among them, thus obliging the Mahatma's biographers to link his beliefs and practices only to the vaguest and most collective of Hindu, Jain or Buddhist influences, while at the same time clearly and individually ascribing Gandhi's debts to European thinkers.[1] For it is all too evident that even the Indian politicians whom he most admired did not provide the Mahatma with any of his models either in the realm of thought or action.

Given the fact that his entire intellectual and political development occurred outside India, first as a student in England and then a lawyer and activist in South Africa, it should come as no surprise that the man who as Mahatma would come to represent all things Indian, was in many ways a stranger to his own country. So when after a quarter of a century spent abroad he returned to India in 1914 as the hero of a non-violent struggle in South Africa, Gandhi was sent on a kind of study tour of the country by his political mentor, Gopal Krishna Gokhale, who was not alone in seeing him as a naïve foreigner whose only knowledge of the land had to do with a couple of obscure principalities in Gujarat. Indeed we shall see in chapter four that the Mahatma even familiarized himself with the great traditions of Hinduism, as embodied for instance in a text like the *Bhagavad-Gita* that was to play such a crucial role in his life, by way of its English translation, and during the time he spent in Britain's imperial capital. So what exactly was Indian about Gandhi, or rather, what exactly did his career owe to India's past?

It is all very well to claim that the Mahatma inherited his major concepts, like *ahimsa* or nonviolence, from the religious beliefs of Jains and Buddhists, or that his practice of non-cooperation was derived from traditional Hindu forms of passive resistance like the *dharna*. However correct these genealogies, they refer to a set of customs and rituals that had rarely if ever assumed a political character in times past, so that with the possible exception of the Swadeshi Movement that was dedicated to the boycott of English manufactures in the early years of the twentieth century, it is impossible to point to any historical example that might provide a precedent for Gandhi's use of them. But without precedents of this kind the Mahatma's politics remain inexplicable in terms of the Indian past, and can only be seen as an irruption into history of some strange and cosmopolitan concoction, whose ingredients were amassed in London, Johannesburg and Bombay. And while it may be quite appropriate to consider Gandhi as being more of an imperial than a national figure, it is in fact possible to link his politics to the Indian past in a manner that is not simply generic.

BASTARD HISTORY

The problem with most attempts to forge such a connection has been their concern with the unspoken requirement to place the Mahatma's politics within some kind of alternative history, a narrative of peace and virtue that could only be linked to the most sublime aspects of India's religious life. But what if Gandhi's ideas and practices emerged instead from a past of conflict and violence? Without denying its cosmopolitan background, therefore, I propose that the Mahatma's politics was not part of any alternative history, but belongs rather to a well-known narrative of warfare and conquest in northern India. In particular I want examine how the Indian Mutiny of 1857, which in military terms marked the greatest crisis of British rule in the Subcontinent, provides the only historical precedent for several of the practices by which Gandhi's politics was known, including non-cooperation, encouraging native manufactures and the working out of a new moral relationship between Hindus and Muslims. Yet this inheritance is a bastard one, since I am not claiming that the Mahatma's politics can be derived directly or legitimately from those of the mutineers, only that their relationship cannot at the same time be ignored either.

Gandhi's own references to the Mutiny were invariably negative, and he saw it much like the British did, as an orgy of violence that degraded both sides in a savage war that he would only with difficulty come to acknowledge as having been fought for India's independence. Indeed in the early years of his career the Mahatma often praised those Indian sepoys who had remained loyal to Britain during the Mutiny, thus making her rule possible despite the ingratitude they were subsequently shown. Although such references ceased once the Mahatma lost faith in the empire around the second decade of the twentieth century, he never displayed any approbation of the Mutiny, even if it had by then become one of the grandest motifs in the historical imagination of Indian nationalism, having been called the country's first war of independence in a famous book by one of

Gandhi's most obdurate foes, the Hindu leader Vinayak Damodar Savarkar, who would eventually be implicated—and acquitted—for conspiring in the Mahatma's assassination.[2]

Having read Kaye and Malleson's voluminous account of the Mutiny while in South Africa, Gandhi should have been familiar with its chief themes, including as they did a dislike of Christian missionary activity and the desire for a partnership between Hindus and Muslims, both concerns that came to constitute important parts of his own struggle.[3] Indeed given the fact that nationalists during his lifetime looked back at the Mutiny as providing an inspiring example of how India's religious communities might unite against colonialism, the Mahatma's silence about this commonly accepted precedent must be acknowledged as being nothing if not pregnant. But having found their political form in the Mutiny as nowhere else in the Indian past, such themes are capable of forcing themselves into the official genealogies of Gandhi's fight for his country's liberation. And my task in this chapter is precisely to put these two narratives together, and in doing so draw the lineaments of a bastard history of nonviolence.

A revolution that wasn't

In the spring of 1857 some of the East India Company's troops in Barrackpore and Berhampore began refusing to follow orders. Rising against the English in Meerut soon after, these soldiers marched to Delhi, where they placed the powerless Mughal emperor, himself a pensioner of the Company, at their head. Spreading across a large portion of northern India, including the cities of Cawnpore and Lucknow, the revolt was eventually put down by men loyal to the British and by the end of 1858 had been completely stamped out. Apart from constituting the greatest anti-colonial rebellion of the nineteenth century, to which Karl Marx, for instance, devoted several essays that compared it to the French Revolution among other historical events, the Indian Mutiny was immediately recognized as a war unprecedented in its brutality, involving as it did massacres of civilians on both sides and the large-scale destruction of their habitations.[4] And though the Mutiny's casualties were not comparable to those of the roughly contemporaneous Crimean War or the Civil War in America, it remained the most important site of cruelty, horror and bloodshed for both Englishmen and Indians at least until the First World War. Indeed for Victorian writers the revolt represented the previously unknown depths to which human beings, whether English or Indian, could sink in the savagery of their passions.[5]

While colonial accounts of the Mutiny, in other words, tended to emphasize its links to and precedents from India's barbarous past, they were also quick to acknowledge the event's utter novelty, not least because of the monstrousness it inspired among the English themselves. In this way the revolt seemed to give the lie to Victorian notions of moral progress by opening up an abyss within human nature itself. For Marx, of course, the rebellion represented a struggle against capitalism's inhumanity, and he saw it as the closest thing to a revolution on the Asian continent. Instead the Indian Mutiny might better be seen as one of the world's first modern wars in its mobilization and targeting of civilians as much as their places of work, residence and recreation, all in violation of moral and legal norms in their British as well as Indian incarnations. For the violence of modern warfare, let us remember, derives from the relatively unregulated character of colonial and civil wars more than it does from the rule-bound conflicts of European dynasties, which have provided us with the laws of war that we flout on every modern battlefield.[6] Nevertheless, in colonial accounts what we might call the Mutiny's modernity continued to be juxtaposed with the elements that it drew from Indian tradition.

Contemporary Indian authors were more likely to see the rebellion as an unprecedented, and in this sense thoroughly modern, event, though they identified as new or strange the very beliefs and practices which for colonial authors signaled the pull of tradition. There was for instance the rumor that newly-issued bullet cartridges which the Company's soldiers were meant to bite open were greased with the fat of cows and pigs to defile Hindus and Muslims. Then there was the anonymous circulation of chapattis, the unleavened bread that is a staple across northern India, which served as omens of an impending attack on the religious obligations of Indians, the forcible breaking of whose dietary taboos would make them into generic individuals capable of becoming undifferentiated slaves of the English. Together with more recognizably "political" claims about the Company's intentions of conquering the remaining Indian kingdoms and reducing their inhabitants to servitude, these fears of being converted to Christianity by the breaching of dietary and other proscriptions should have been familiar to Indian writers of the time, but what interested them was the way in which such charges had been transformed in the rebellion, seen as an event unknown to previous history. So it is not surprising that Indian writers quickly identified the Mutiny with the kind of historical break that characterized modernity in its European sense.

Arguments about the Mutiny's modernity have for a long time now been retailed by Indian and Pakistani nationalists, who view the revolt as in some way a precursor of their respective independence movements. But this is a thesis that derives no clear support from Indian documents of the period, instead finding its origins in British texts on the revolt, for instance in the lengthy summation by the Judge-Advocate at the trial of the Mughal emperor, known to his prosecutors as the ex-King of Delhi. Referring to the rebellious troops of the East India Company, this gentleman averred that it was British rule that had created among them the potential for unity and even of a European form of nationality:

Brahman and Mussulman here met as it were upon neutral ground; they have had, in the army, one common brotherhood of profession, the same dress, the same rewards, the same objects to be arrived at by the same means. They frequently joined each other in their separate festivals, and the union encouraged by the favor of the Government was finally resorted to as a measure to subvert it.[7]

Whatever the merits of this oft-repeated argument, in which we might recognize the origins of nationalism in the Subcontinent, it finds some confirmation in contemporary Indian accounts of the Mutiny like that of the famous Muslim reformer Sayyid Ahmad Khan.[8] Indeed most Indian accounts of the rebellion are full of statements about its novelty, with the events of 1857 made comparable only with the most distant and momentous of precedents, ranging from the Arab conquest of Persia to the *Réconquista* in Spain.[9] But what interests me here are not the historical analogies drawn by commentators of the time so much as the issues that gave the revolt its language: cartridges, chapattis, conversion and the king who was meant to save his subjects from all three. These are the very elements that for colonial and nationalist writers tie the Indian Mutiny back to tradition and the past.

With their highly pluralistic rhetoric about preserving religious distinctions and their fear of the uniformity resulting from conversion to Christianity, the rebels can be said to represent the struggle of an empire against a nation rather than the reverse. Even so hostile a writer as Sayyid Ahmad Khan, who published the first Indian account of the Mutiny in 1859, recognized the rebels' fear of such unity when he described, for example, the controversial letters penned by an English missionary in 1855 arguing for a single religion in a country that had been unified under a single government by means of the telegraph, railways and roads.[10] However this empire of the imagination that was the Mutiny's ideal belonged not to the Subcontinent's past but its future, informing political movements there into our own times. To reveal the outlines of this new empire I shall focus on three kinds of documents from the revolt's vast archive: trial transcripts from the Mutiny's opening salvos in Barrackpore and its closing scenes in Delhi, some texts of rebel proclamations throughout this period and a few contemporary accounts of these events by Indian writers.

Biting the bullet

The correspondence and court transcripts from the Mutiny's beginnings in Barrackpore and Berhampore all put into question the sepoys' belief in rumors concerning the new cartridges they were meant to bite open, as well as their responsibility in fomenting rebellion within the Bengal Army. Even taking into account any British inclination to blame dark forces beyond their army for the revolt, these documents are unambiguous in pointing out the skepticism of many soldiers regarding the cartridge rumors. Thus Lieutenant and Brevet-Captain J.A. Wright, commanding the Rifle Instruction Depot, wrote to the depot adjutant at Dum Dum on 22 January:

Some of the depot men, in conversing with me on the subject last night, said that the report has spread throughout India, and when they go to their homes their friends will refuse to eat with them. I assured them (believing it to be the case) that the grease used is composed of mutton fat and wax; to which they replied—"it may be so, but our friends will not believe it; let us obtain the ingredients from the bazar and make it up ourselves; we shall then know what is used, and be able to assure our fellow soldiers and others that there is nothing in it prohibited by our caste".[11]

This is only one of a number of accounts of Indian soldiers respectfully asking their English superiors to permit them to grease the cartridges with ingredients of their own choice. And while each such request attributes belief in rumors of pollution to the soldiers' friends and family, the sepoys often went to the length of testing the cartridges themselves to see if they contained animal fat—though they seem not to have objected to the use of mutton and other grease. Here is a fairly typical example from the testimony of Havildar-Major Ajoodiah Singh, from the 8th Company of the 2nd Regiment Native (Grenadier) Infantry, at a special court of inquiry held at Barrackpore on 6 February:

Question: Have you any objection to the use of the cartridges lying on the table?

Answer: I have suspicions about the paper on account of the bazar report that there is grease in it.

Question: Have you taken any measures to prove whether this report is true?

Answer: I have tried it in oil and also in water. And where it was wet with the oil it would not dissolve; after this trial I thought there was no grease in it.

Question: By the experiment, in your opinion, there was no grease in the paper; would you object to bite off the end of the cartridge?

Answer: I could not do it, as the other men would object to it.[12]

Pursuing the "bazaar rumor" that seemed to have struck their army with the fear of being ostracized by its own countrymen, British officers were quick to blame outside agents for it, including the recently-deposed King of Oudh, but more especially Brahmin and Hindu organizations in Calcutta that were angered by the Company's legalization of widow remarriage and proscription of *sati* or widow burning.[13] Indeed the courts of inquiry convened during the initial stages of the mutiny determined that it was the Hindu soldiers alone who were disloyal and untrustworthy, with Muslims and Sikhs being judged responsible and reliable.[14] And this despite the fact that the rumors of greased cartridges spoke from the very beginning of their contamination by cow and pig fat to pollute Hindus and Muslims both. So at the trial of the ex-King of Delhi in 1858, Captain Martineau of the 10th Native Infantry only echoed the general opinion when he dismissed Muslim concern with the contamination of cartridges:

Question: Did you observe any difference in making complaints about forcible deprivation of their religion between the Hindu and the Mussulman?

Answer: Yes, as far as the cartridge question went the Mahommedan sepoys laughed at it; it was only the Hindus that made the complaints in reference to losing caste; but in regard to those who spoke of the annexation of Oudh as a grievance I can't say whether they were Mahommedans or not.[15]

The Judge-Advocate at the King's trial relied upon such testimony to dismiss the earlier judgment of his colleagues in Barrackpore and argue that the Mutiny had been a Muslim plot, with its Hindu supporters serving merely as tools in the hands of Bahadur Shah and his accomplices. What is striking in all this, however, is the fact that neither Hindu nor Muslim soldiers appeared to have believed in the cartridge rumors, claiming rather that they were protesting on behalf of others, anonymous Indians whose opinion put the sepoys, their friends and families at risk of ostracism. Whether or not this anonymous and possibly non-existent host may be seen as a nation in waiting, important about the mutineers' rhetoric was its disavowal of any personal belief for the obligation owed others. In other words there was no presumption of any shared faith in such rhetoric, only the duty subsisting between these soldiers and their kith and kin.

Notwithstanding the absence of individual or collective faith in mutinous rhetoric among many of the sepoys, this lack being compensated for by a sense of individual and collective obligation, striking about the early days of the revolt were the soldiers' respectful requests of their superiors, together with principled refusals to follow their orders. We have to wait more than sixty years to see similar forms of moral protest in India, this time under the name of Gandhi's non-cooperation. This reference to the Mahatma is not a throwaway one, as throughout the course of their revolt we find the sepoys asking Indians in general, rather than those belonging to the same caste or locality, to refuse to work for the British, thus creating the only historical precedent we have for Gandhi's country-wide practice of "truth-force" or *satyagraha*.[16] And yet we shall see that the mutineers refused at the same time to subordinate their caste and religious distinctions to some undifferentiated notion of being Indian, this kind of uniformity being precisely what they feared from British rule. And though historians have often seen such distinctions as confining rebel politics to pre-modern status, we will see in the following chapters that it was exactly a faith in these distinctions that marked the Mahatma's politics as well. So it should come as no surprise to note that the following rebel proclamation appears to prefigure Gandhi's politics by going so far as to discount a military victory over the British and recommend instead non-cooperation of an entirely civilian kind:

"Consider yourselves dead even before death". This alone can save you. Otherwise you will be bought over by their allurement and then put to death. There will be no chance of escape; all will have cause to repent, and will bite their fingers with their teeth when repentance will be of no avail. If you think they have no army, that their hopes are gone and their ambitions frustrated, such an idea is delusive. Consider what an army they have between Cawnpore and Calcutta. They are on friendly terms with all the European powers—these in the hour of misfortune readily help each other. If you too are all united and refuse to accept appointments of any kind under them, they will be reduced to despair. There is a fable that a woodcutter came to a certain grove of trees and the trees said "Lo! Here is our enemy, but we need not fear as he can not harm us". But when they saw a wooden handle affixed to his axe they said "alas! One of our tribe has joined him, now we may bid farewell to all our liberty".[17]

Whether or not they believed in bazaar rumors about cartridges and chapattis, what the mutineers were protesting was the threat that British attempts to unify them posed the moral imagination structuring north Indian society as an empire of distinctions. It was this threat that came to be symbolized by cartridges and chapattis, with Captain Martineau describing the latter at the ex-King's trial in the following way:

I asked them what they understood in reference to them, and by whom they supposed that they were circulated: they described them to me as being in size and shape like ship biscuits, and believed them to have been distributed by order of Government through the medium of their servants for the purpose of intimating to the people of Hindustan that they should be all compelled to eat the same food: and that was considered as a token, that they would likewise be compelled to embrace one faith, or as they termed it, "One food and one faith".[18]

In its edition of 5 July 1857, the *Dehli Urdu Akhbar*, a newspaper sympathetic to the mutineers, elaborated upon this attitude by describing the fear of conversion as a loss of selfhood that was tantamount to slavery:

Everybody's faith would be polluted and they would be expelled from their communities and they would not be allowed to eat or sit or intermingle or intermarry with their compatriots and communities. They should lose their children, wives, friends and strangers and they should not have anyone to call their own in all of Hindustan except for the English. So that ultimately, they have no choice but to accept the Christian faith. That their fate should be tied to the goras [whites] and they should spend their lives, energy and fortune in defending the English annexation—just as it has been heard that at Agra all the Christians have sided with the English and they every day acquire military training and are committed with all their might and money.[19]

Without limits and distinctions, moral action itself was impossible along with a moral actor who was something more than an abstraction. Thus rebels accused the English not of keeping aloof from Indians so much as of trying to convert them into their own society. And this vision of a population rendered uniform through conversion suggested to the mutineers only a state of enslavement, though it was clear to them that accepting Christianity would earn them favor. It was in this sense that the Mutiny represented an empire of distinctions, one in which differences between rulers and subjects as well as among these subjects were much to be desired because they made morality possible in the form of obligation towards others. Indeed the mutineers feared not the violation of their religion, as the English translation of the day would have it, but rather of their moral duty, called *dharma* in Sanskrit and *farz* in Arabic. One of the rebel proclamations, issued in the name of Bahadur Shah, even went so far as to quote a verse of the *Bhagavad-Gita* on how it was preferable to die than forsake one's own duty for that of another.[20]

The British were therefore accused by the rebels of being indiscriminate not only about the things they ate, but also by dint of their sexual voraciousness and indifference to breaches of promise and trust—the same kinds of accusations that were habitually leveled at low caste individuals and rivals of all sorts. But while this refusal to draw distinctions and set limits to their behavior might be tolerated among undistinguished persons, it was dangerous in the English because they now ruled India and were so expected to act in a manner that befitted their station. These obligations were important, in other words, because rulers had the power to corrupt their subjects and indeed the state itself by such immoral practices.[21] Now all this might seem very traditional, as indeed it is, until we recall that the Mutiny also served as a founding moment for the widespread fears of conversion as well as the disputes over it that exist to this day between Christians, Muslims and Hindus—to say nothing about Indians themselves adopting such European forms of proselytism in order to breach the obligations they owe their neighbors. Such "traditional" views regarding the corrupting influence of rulers or the immorality of conversion came to the fore once again in Gandhi's politics.

The rebels did not accuse the British of being inherently wicked and therefore did not entertain a racial view of them, or rather one in which such wickedness was seen as being part of their national character. This lack of concern with the Englishness of their enemies was demonstrated by the fact that the mutineers tended to spare any who claimed to have converted to Islam—conversion to Hinduism being of course impossible in that period. Odd about this fact is that even bizarre claims, including those by women and children feigning to be Kashmiris, seem to have been accepted at face value as a kind of courtesy, as if to prove that it was not conversion the rebels objected to so much as the duplicitous and engineered proselytization feared of the British. And indeed both Englishmen and Indians at the time discounted any concern with conversion on the part of the sepoys, with Sayyid Ahmad Khan pointing out that while everyone in India was free to preach his religion, Christian missionaries were the only ones to force their often insulting sermons upon others not only in public places like markets, but also at Hindu and Muslim festivals and sites of pilgrimage.[22] The Brahmin author of a Marathi account of the Mutiny similarly tells us that its Muslim supporters were anxious to distinguish conversion to Islam from that to Christianity, minimizing the former's importance and condemning the anti-Hindu policies of the eighteenth century Mughal emperor Aurangzeb as a disastrous precedent for British evangelism.[23] This distinction between coerced and hospitable forms of proselytism became a standard one after the Mutiny, with Gandhi himself upholding it, and it is a distinction that continues to be invoked today by popular opinion as much as anti-conversion legislation in various parts of India and Pakistan.

The English therefore do not seem to have been disliked for being foreigners at all, but only for breaking the moral compact that defined India as an empire of distinctions. So Sayyid Ahmad Khan pointed out that his countrymen could have no objection to be ruled by aliens of one sort or another since this had for centuries been the regular state of affairs for the majority,[24] and that furthermore Indians were used to flocking to the banner of whichever power promised to become dominant and maintain a moral compact with them.[25] This argument reappears with Gandhi, who was adamant in making the point that the British were to be fought not as aliens but rather as unfit rulers. Thus he was willing at least in his early career to countenance India's participation in the empire, while being unwilling to accept any definition of independence that would simply replace English faces with Indian ones. Precedents for the Mahatma's vision of imperialism as a moral compact having nothing to do with race are evident in mutineers' texts, such as the following passages from the "Advice of the Royal Army":

It has been handed down by tradition that dominion is retained by one individual, only because it is the gift of God; and that this divine gift only lasts and prospers so long as the holder performs his duties with gratitude and thanksgiving. An instance of the truth of this is the English rule in India; as almighty God has said in the Holy Quran: "Upon whomsoever we confer a bounty, we do not wrest from him until he alters his habits". [...] There were three causes which contributed to the success of the British rule in India.

1. They were true to their promises and engagements.
2. They did much service by the construction of roads and earned the gratitude of travellers by ensuring their safety.
3. In administering justice they showed no partiality to members of their own tribe.[26]

Misgovernment, oppression, breaking of treaties, evil intentions, bigotry, bitter animosity towards natives of India, pride, blasphemous arrogance—a single one of these bad qualities would suffice for the subversion of an empire—but as it happens all of them are concentrated in the English character.[27]

In the absence of a racial or even dynastic conception of rule, a moral compact provided the only framework within which to judge misrule, which is perhaps why acts of English perfidy like the annexation of Oudh were seen by many of the mutineers not as causes for revolt in any patriotic let alone religious sense but merely as examples of British bad faith. Thus witnesses at the ex-King's trial insisted that the sepoys had little interest in or loyalty to the king and territory of Oudh. And Ahsanullah Khan, the ex-King's physician, not only claimed that the Sunnis of Delhi regarded Oudh's annexation as divine punishment for its Shia ruler's persecution of their fellow sectarians,[28] but also that the mutinous soldiers saw the event as an example of treachery without being particularly enraged by the annexation. "The sepoys who were at Delhi never complained particularly against the annexation of Oudh. But they certainly used to say that the British would take possession of every province as they had occupied Oudh; and that they took possession of that country even though the King did not fight against them".[29]

Here and there the imperial theory of rule represented by a moral compact was modernized in mutineer rhetoric by the recognition of contemporary realities both political and economic. Thus the strained British relations with Russia, Persia and Afghanistan provided the basis for expectations of military support from these quarters. More interesting, however, was the rebels' recognition that the Company's economic power differed from and indeed rivaled the political authority represented by Queen Victoria, who is described in the following excerpt from a mutinous pamphlet both as an example of English immorality, and as a fellow-victim of the East India Company driven into the hands of Britain's traditional enemy France by the hand of her foreign husband:

It so happened that the Emperor of the French sent a message to the Queen by her husband and this secret having transpired, the English had a council at which it was unanimously determined that her husband was never to be admitted to her presence in future unless four men were present on the occasion. As a last resort and in order to quench the fire of lust, the Queen has now selected an Ethiopian boy who is anxious to carry her off to Africa. Victoria has all but yielded to the proposition as she cannot bear to be separated from him and it is confidently expected that in the end she will become a fakir and abdicate the throne. The Company is desirous of wresting the Kingdom from Victoria in the same way as they wrested the Kingdom of Oude from its sovereign.[30]

BASTARD HISTORY

However garbled it might appear in their pronouncements, the mutineers appear to have possessed a firm enough grasp of contemporary reality to belie any assertion that they were simply traditional rebels. The Mutiny's novelty, however, should not be identified in standard colonial or nationalist fashion, merely by recognizing the undeniable Europeanization of its soldiers in the matter of training, organization or even consciousness. It is another kind of future that this momentous event inaugurates, one that is discernible in the supposedly old-fashioned relations it created between Hindus and Muslims on the one hand and between subjects and their king on the other.

Tweedledum and Tweedledee

The earliest rumors about greased cartridges are said to have emanated from a low caste military employee at Barrackpore who asked a Brahmin soldier for water, and upon being refused it disclosed that the British were planning to destroy the caste of both Hindus and Muslims. Here is one account of the rumor as reported by Major General J.B. Hearsey, commanding the Presidency Division, to Colonel R.J.H. Birch, Secretary to the Government of India in the Military Department, dated 11 February 1857:

> A sepoy from one of the regiments here was walking to his chowka [compound] to prepare his food, with his lota [vessel], full of water. He was met by a low-caste khalasi [laborer] (it is said to be one of the magazine or arsenal men). This khalasi asked him to let him drink from the lota. The sepoy, a Brahmin, refused saying—"I have scoured my lota; you will defile it by your touch". The khalasi rejoined—"you think much of your caste, but wait a little, the saheb-logue [British] will make you bite cartridges soaked in cow and pork fat, and then where will your caste be?"[31]

Let us note a couple of peculiarities in this account: for one thing a Brahmin would have had no religious objection in pouring out some water for any low caste or indeed Muslim individual to drink—only to handing either one the drinking vessel. And for another, Muslims would not have had any religious objection in handing a drinking vessel to such a person. In other words the symmetry set up in this account and all others like it between Hindus and Muslims is a false one both theoretically and historically. We have already seen how Muslim sepoys laughed at the idea of being polluted by the cartridges. Thus Sayyid Ahmad Khan points out that had Hindus and Muslims not been put together in the same units, the latter would very likely have had no objection in biting the cartridges.[32] Indeed he traced this habit of dutiful solidarity with one's neighbor to earlier protests against the provision of food in jails, where cooks of lower caste ended up polluting many Hindu prisoners, and in doing so hurting their Muslim neighbors though they had no religious objection to such food themselves.[33]

As for the caste hierarchy whose subversion this rumor of polluted food announces, we hear nothing more about it in Mutiny documents. The low-caste herald of British perfidy appears in the story only to set up a symmetrical relationship between high-caste Hindus and wellborn Muslims, promptly to disappear after serving his role as the outsider from whose point of view alone could these groups appear comparable. This suggests that the rebels were occupied in their rhetoric with conceiving of an entirely new kind of Hindu-Muslim relationship, one that depended on the myth of symmetry between the two. Now this kind of symmetry had been invoked by mystics and poets in the past, but only to be condemned, since it was understood as representing the similarity between equally bigoted men of religion. It was the *brahmin* and the *shaykh*, therefore, rather than Hindus and Muslims, who had previously been so compared. Even when viewed favorably, this religious similarity was seen merely as the sign of a deeper and truer unity, generally embodied by a mystical figure standing outside the bounds of religious doctrine. Instead of following the mystic script and abandoning such symmetry for a deeper unity, however, rebel rhetoric actually dispensed with the saintly figure positioned outside this relationship, whose place was now occupied by low-caste individuals and Englishmen. Or to put it in other words, the mystical union of religions was ignored to establish moral and political relations between them.

Though mutineer texts urge Hindus and Muslims to unite in fighting the common threat that the British posed, it is clear that they were by no means meant to fight as one people. On the contrary rebel rhetoric seems obsessed by working out a new relationship between Hindus and Muslims in which each is meant to sacrifice their own interest for the other's religious scruples without sharing these in any way—thus relating to one another in the same way that we have seen the sepoys related to their friends and families. Instead of being related to one another by loyalty to the king, as had been the case with religious and ethnic groups in times past, Hindus and Muslims had now to create a new model of interaction, one which found its origin in the rebel army. And indeed Bahadur Shah seems never to have claimed the sepoys' loyalty either for himself or for his dynasty but rather in the name of their own religions. Here is a passage elaborating this new relationship from a proclamation attributed to the King, the first part recounting an English plot to destroy the caste duty of Hindus and the second proposing a moral compact between Hindus and Muslims:

They accordingly now ordered the Brahmans and others of their army to bite cartridges in the making up of which fat had been used. The Mussulman soldiers perceived that by this expedient the religion of the Brahmans and Hindus only was in danger, but nevertheless they also refused to bite them. [...] The slaughter of kine is regarded by the Hindus as a great insult to their religion. To prevent this, a solemn compact or agreement has been entered into by all the Mahommedan chiefs of Hindustan, binding themselves that if the Hindus will come forward to slay the English, the Mahommedans will from that very day put a stop to the slaughter of cows, and those of them who will not do so, will be considered to have abjured the Kuran, and such of them as will eat beef will be regarded as though they had eaten pork: but if the Hindus will not gird their loins to kill the English, but will try to save them, they will be as guilty in the sight of God as though they had committed the sins of killing cows and eating flesh.[34]

Again we see the attempt to create relations of symmetry between the adherents of India's two dominant religions. Such efforts possessed a long history in Mughal India but were transformed by the revolt into a pact of mutual sacrifice and defense for the first time. While the passage above appears to suggest that Hindus needed to be cajoled into rebellion by Muslims, which was exactly the conclusion drawn by the Judge-Advocate in the ex-King of Delhi's trial, we know that the majority of mutinous sepoys were in fact Hindus. This proclamation, then, might indicate that some Muslims at least had come to recognize the necessity of Hindu support in any movement to topple and replace the British. The anxiety produced by such a recognition is evident in this and other Muslim offers to come to a religious understanding with their Hindu neighbors, since these would-be pacts are sometimes followed by acknowledgements that the English might themselves come to similar arrangements with Hindus and leave Muslims out in the cold.[35]

Muslim offers of a religious pact in which they promised to abjure cow slaughter, and the anxious recognition that Hindu support was required to achieve Islam's freedom in India, both resurfaced in the aftermath of the First World War. Many Indian Muslims then feared for the titles and territories of the defeated Ottomans, whose sultan also claimed to be the Caliph or spiritual head of Sunni Islam. The agitation these men began against the Allied partition of Ottoman lands was joined by the Indian National Congress under Gandhi's inspiration, and it was to the Mahatma that Muslim divines made their offers of a compact, only to be met with a firm refusal of any deal. Like a number of his predecessors during the Mutiny, Gandhi made it clear that such an alliance was not a worldly and therefore temporary contract, but instead a relationship made up of sacrifices offered by one party in defense of another's religious prejudices. So he approved the apparently irrational cause of the Caliphate, because separated from any politics of rational interest it demonstrated the purely religious or idealistic motives of India's Muslims and could therefore form the basis of an equally disinterested relationship with their Hindu neighbors. For whatever the truth of the matter, the Mahatma realized that a nation could not come into being by a calculus of interests but only by way of a mobilization that was truly idealistic in character. I shall explore Gandhi's participation in this movement at greater length in chapter three.

Even as it was happening, the Khilafat (Caliphate) agitation was routinely compared to the Mutiny, not only due to the new religious relations it had created, but also because it was the only event to pose a comparable threat to the British Empire. Just as Muslim soldiers in 1857 were said to have supported Hindu concerns about ritual pollution without themselves believing in such a thing, so too did Hindus under the Mahatma's leadership support the cause of the Caliphate. And if Gandhi's Muslim allies made him into the "dictator" of the Khilafat Movement and forbade cow-slaughter even on their feast of sacrifice, they were only following the precedent set by their ancestors during the revolt in Delhi, as reported by one of the city's English survivors, Mrs Aldwell, at the ex-King's trial:

Question: Had the Mussulmans and Hindus had quarrels or discussions among themselves on the score of religion when they were in Delhi together?

Answer: I think when the troops first came, the Hindus made the King promise that there should be no oxen killed in the city, and this promise was kept. I believe that not a single ox was killed in Delhi during the whole time of the rebellion. On the festival of the Bakr-Eed, when the Mahommedans usually slaughter an ox, a disturbance was expected; but the Mahommedans refrained from doing so on this occasion.[36]

If this arrangement looks very much like a worldly contract, its sacrificial nature was demonstrated in the breakdown of inter-religious agreement once the tide started turning against the mutineers. In the words of Mrs Aldwell, "The Hindu sepoys especially upbraided the Mahommedans, saying: "This is your first engagement with the English; is this the way you intend to fight for your faith?" They also already spoke in terms of much regret of the turn that affairs had taken, reproached the Mahommedans for having deceived them on pretenses of their religion, and seemed to doubt greatly whether the English Government had really had any intention of interfering with their caste".[37]

Just like the failure of the Mutiny before it, that of the Khilafat Movement in 1922 led to a great deal of acrimony among Hindus and Muslims, each community accusing the other of duplicity as far as its professions of disinterested friendship were concerned. But in either case this only confirms the sheer originality of the failed effort to create a new kind of relationship between these adherents of the Subcontinent's two major religions. Indians commonly attributed the failure of both these movements to their breaking of the moral compact they were meant to protect. In the case of Khilafat, it was the Mahatma who put a stop to the movement once its supporters turned to violence. And in that of the Mutiny, ordinary Indians seem to have dissociated themselves from the rebels once their violence departed moral norms. Of course these disapproving Indians were not an undifferentiated or disinterested lot, and nationalist historians have made much of the mutineers' supposed betrayal by Hindu and Muslim elites, both aristocrats and merchants, whose power they threatened. Like their colonial predecessors, nationalist writers have also blamed the Mutiny's failure upon the rebels' inability to extricate themselves from inherited patterns of hierarchical thinking. Whatever the validity of such arguments, the moral compact that defined the Revolt's empire of distinctions is noteworthy, not least because it represented no tradition but a new historical departure.

BASTARD HISTORY

It is true that many among the gentry deplored the rise to power of the mutinous army, one that ruled in its own name and followed no royal house or religious authority, despite its forcible adoption of Bahadur Shah as leader. The following passage from a memoir of the revolt in Delhi is typical in its contempt for the radically new social form taken by the soldiers:

> An upheaval of newly risen men occurred, and a group of them rose like a plague; a different creation, (men whose) manner was different, whose style differed, whose way was disagreeable [...] and whose signs differed; (men) whose community was new, various sorts of men whose habits were several. To sum up, such (men) were gathered who possessed neither the mark of shame on their foreheads nor the style of loyalty in their human makeup. Where was chivalry? Where courage? If some afflicted one saluted (them), they would move hands as if broken (in returning the greeting), and with contempt furthermore. If some needy one opened the mouth of supplication, they would, like the dumb, not reply, or if they did, villainously. Because of selfishness, most of them do not accept any superior, and by reason of pride most consider themselves better than anyone else.[38]

The rebel army convened its own councils, appointed its own generals and marched under some version of the motto *khalq-e khuda, mulk-e padishah, hukm-e sipah* (to God belongs creation, to the Emperor his country and command to the soldier). The sepoys themselves seem to have mistrusted many among their aristocratic allies, of whom there were in fact very few, with none of India's leading princes lending the mutineers their support. This mistrust expressed itself in fears that Mughal courtiers had reached an understanding with the English to betray the rebels, this being the reason why they were protecting the lives of British women and children who had taken refuge in the palace. Despite the remonstrance of the royal physician and at least one prince, these hostages were massacred on 16 May 1857, to the horror of Delhi's citizens. As Chuni Lal the newswriter reported, "After the slaughter the bodies were laden on two carts, and thrown into the river. This occurrence caused a great excitement amongst the Hindus throughout the city, who said that these Purbeas [easterners] who had committed this heinous and atrocious cruelty could never be victorious against the English".[39]

The mutineers, in other words, were castigated for breaking the moral compact they sought to defend, and contemporary writers, wellborn to a man, accused them precisely of this offence. Here is an account of rebel crimes by Bahadur Shah, who had tried without much success to ensure that some semblance of law and order was maintained in Delhi during sepoy rule:

> Moreover without reference to night or day, they enter and plunder the houses of the inhabitants on the false plea that they have concealed Europeans. They force locks and shop-doors and openly carry away the property from the shops, and they forcibly loose the horses of the cavalry and take them off. They commit these excesses in the face of the fact that all cities taken without military operations have ever been exempted from sack and slaughter. Even Jangiz Khan and Nadir Shah, kings execrated as tyrants, gave peace and protection to such cities as surrendered without resistance.[40]

However well intended, these desires and efforts to restore stability in rebel territory all seem rather old-fashioned compared with the undeniable modernity of mutineer practices, which included the unheard of publication of collective pronouncements in the name of the army to its brothers and unprecedented calls to mobilize women, children and the elderly for warfare. Nevertheless, these very proclamations also promised Indians of various classes a restoration of traditional regulations concerning widow burning and remarriage, noble inheritances and the like.[41] Furthermore they promised the elimination of taxes on large landholders, the waiving of British trade monopolies, stamp fees and customs duties upon merchants, the offer of better salaries and the possibility of advancement to the highest ranks for soldiers and public servants, the proscription of English manufactures and guarantee of employment for artisans at the courts and estates of the aristocracy, and the granting of rent-free lands for pundits and fakirs.[42] This recourse to tradition can be seen as atavistic or opportunistic in its recognition of the complaints that various classes of Indians entertained against British rule, though it might equally herald the origins of *swadeshi*, the nationalist movement in favor of abandoning British manufactures to encourage Indian artisanship that achieved its culmination with Gandhi. Below I shall examine how the Mutiny redefined traditional authority altogether—beginning with that of the king.

Authority without power

The mutineers might have had good military cause for taking Delhi, and their propping up of Bahadur Shah as emperor may have possessed an equally sound political rationale, but the consequences of his elevation went well beyond such logistical reasoning. While the enthronement of puppet kings was a familiar enough event, with Bahadur Shah having occupied precisely this position from the beginning of his reign, the King's role during the revolt assumed an altogether different countenance. From being a petitioner and pensioner of the East India Company, he suddenly became a figure of moral rather than royal authority. Even before the Mutiny, of course, this scion of a long decrepit dynasty had enjoyed a curious significance among India's great princes, each one richer and more powerful than himself. The royal physician Ahsanullah Khan said as much to the court trying his former master. "The King was a personage to wait upon whom all Chiefs, Hindu or Mahomedan, would have considered an honor to themselves".[43]

But to attribute this authority to some legitimacy inherited from the heyday of Mughal rule does not tell us much, especially given the well-known humiliations that the House of Timur had been subjected to by its successive protectors, of whom the British were only the last. It was not therefore the much-tarnished sanctity of Bahadur Shah's dynasty that lent him any superstitious legitimacy, but what we might perhaps call the constitutional position he occupied, one that was augmented by his very powerlessness. Very briefly, I would like to suggest that this position had to do with a declining dynasty's neutrality within India's ethnic, religious and indeed political landscape. Unlike the Rajputs, Afghans, Sikhs or Marathas after all, the Mughals possessed neither regional nor ethno-linguistic partisans among their subjects, their own tribe of Chagatay Turks being too insignificant in number to provide one. Such ties as they had were with groups like the Rajputs among whom the emperors married. Furthermore the Mughals' adherence to Islam may have legitimized them among Muslims both in India and abroad, constituting therefore a factor in their empire's international if not domestic standing, but it did not provide a foundation for the dynasty itself. For this was traced back to pre-Islamic times and indeed to a Mongol goddess, to say nothing of including heroes like Hulagu Khan who had conquered Muslim Baghdad and killed its last caliph. So when in its issue of 14 June 1857, the *Dehli Urdu Akhbar* called for a jihad against the British, it did not hesitate to accuse the latter of behaving as proudly as the caliphs of old, and thus deserving the divine punishment meted out to them at the hand of the mutineers, just as their predecessors had been laid low by the Mongols.[44] If the English could be compared to much-revered Muslim rulers in the past and their Indian enemies to Mongol infidels, then it is clear that while the Mughals were certainly viewed as a Muslim dynasty, though in the post-Mongol fashion they recognized no caliph, they cannot be described as an Islamic one.

It was the House of Timur's constitutional if not political neutrality, then, that I would hazard made it into India's only imperial dynasty, with the Maratha, Persian, Afghan and Sikh rulers who effectively succeeded the Mughals all acknowledging their peculiar authority, as indeed did the British themselves throughout the eighteenth century. This neutrality had to do with the fact that the dynasty's legitimacy resided in elements like a half-mythical Mongol ancestry that had little if anything to do with India or its various peoples. And yet this Mongol past did not by any means represent some tribal or regional interest within the empire, not only because the Mughals possessed no such basis, but also because the Mongol theory of rule from which they drew acknowledged no such limitation to begin with. Apart from founding history's greatest empire, the Mongols were the first to conceive its potential as world-encompassing in nature, this limitless vision finding its pale reflection in the grandiloquent titles of world-conqueror (Jahangir), world-emperor (Shah Jahan) and the like used by the Mughals. The House of Timur, in other words, was neutral precisely because it claimed a universality that had nothing to do with region or religion.[45] The Mughals had established this form of imperial authority in the days of Akbar, but what we might call its constitutional aspect was only augmented as the dynasty declined. Indeed the more power it lost the more authority did the House of Timur gain, which is perhaps why Bahadur Shah and his predecessors for several generations had insisted so strongly upon the maintenance of what the British often considered absurd rituals and the formalities of protocol. Rather than illustrating the pathetic attachment of a washed-out monarchy to its vanished greatness, this insistence should perhaps be recognized as crucial to the constitutional status of the Mughals within Indian society, having little if anything to do with the British themselves. So Ahsanullah Khan tells us that Bahadur Shah welcomed news of the rebellion in its early stages only because he thought it would bring to power new rulers who would treat him with greater consideration:

I do not remember exactly the month in which intelligence was received of the regiment near Calcutta having refused to receive the new cartridges. I only know that the information was obtained from a Calcutta newspaper;

and when it was known that the discussion about the cartridges was spreading, it was remarked that, inasmuch as the matter touched the religion of the people, the excitement would spread extensively over the entire length and breadth of the country, and the native army would desert the British Government, whose rule would then be at an end. The King remarked that he would, in that case, be placed in better circumstances, inasmuch as a new dominant power would treat him with greater respect and consideration. The princes of the royal family used to remark that the native army would go over either to Nepal or Persia. But they had no idea that they would unite with the King, because he had neither money nor troops.[46]

Not only Bahadur Shah, but many of his subjects, too, expected that India's new rulers, thought to be Persians for the most part, would set him up as titular emperor in this strictly constitutional sense, rather than seek to transfer power into his hands. So a Delhi newspaper, the *Authentic News*, dated 19 March 1857, compares the king to his ancestor Humayun, who had been helped by the Safavid emperor Shah Abbas to regain his throne. "Why would Hindus welcome the King of Persia? Only if he were to place our own King, as Abbas Shah Safi did Humayun—as it was Timur who gave sovereignty to the Persians".[47] Important about this passage is the fact that it attributes Hindu but not Muslim loyalty to the Mughal emperor, thus demonstrating the dynasty's post-Islamic as well as its neutral character. And it was this neutrality that the emperor repeatedly tried to assert during the Mutiny, as for instance when a spy for the British reported that on 16 August 1857, he kept the arms of rebels fleeing the city, saying, "I do not care who goes or stays, I did not ask anybody to come here and I do not stop anyone, nor prevent anyone from leaving. Whoever wants to stay can do so, otherwise they can go away, I have no objections. I have detained these arms so that if the English come here I can hand it over to them. If the troops want them, they can take them, I have no stake in the matter".[48]

That the mutineers did not join forces with a strong monarch but rushed to Delhi and put themselves under Bahadur Shah's constitutional authority was something nobody expected, for in doing so the rebels not only followed the precedent set by Marathas or Afghans before them, but also broke it by offering their new sovereign no powerful leader to protect him. So while the sepoys treated Bahadur Shah with what must have been a familiar mixture of respect and contempt, they also made him into much more than a constitutional figure, since it was now the King himself who in a tragic restoration most prejudicial to his constitutional status was thrust to the forefront of affairs. Yet in appointing officers, disbursing funds, protecting subjects or remonstrating with his mutinous army, the last Mughal of his line behaved not in the least like an emperor. Instead he tried to enforce his authority by pleading and cajoling, threatening to abdicate his throne, become an ascetic and even commit suicide. In other words this frail and powerless figure had become a moral authority of an altogether novel kind, as the *Dehli Urdu Akhbar* recognized in its edition of 14 August 1857:

> This King of ours is one of the leading saints of the era who has been approved of by the divine court. He spent years upon years, virtually in British imprisonment, never relented, and he never exhorted or incited anyone, never did he covet the throne or riches. Now of its own this divine boon has come his way. He seems bent on retiring and going to the holy places in a mendicant's garb. What has happened so far and what goes on is done entirely by the God-given army. In reality, the King, even then was helpless and content to spend his life in a quiet corner and is now a prisoner in their [the sepoys'] hands. God Almighty helps our King in every situation. It is incumbent on the army and the people to consider the approval of the King as akin to the approval of God and his Prophet and they should not come under the awe or deception of the British—what they acquired was done either through fraud or by breaking their contract.[49]

His physician elaborated upon Bahadur Shah's moral position during his trial, going so far as to say that the ex-King of Delhi had not emphasized it enough when trying, for instance, to save the English women and children held captive in the palace from massacre. "If the King had kept the women and children in his own female apartments, and on their being demanded by the sepoys had explained to the latter that he would only agree to their (the Christians) being murdered, after his (the King's) own women and children had been first put to death, it was very probable that the sepoys would not have dared to enter the royal seraglio to forcibly seize and kill the Christians".[50] What sort of leadership was this in which a powerless king ruled by the rhetoric of sacrifice? Had India seen such a monarch before other than in the pages of books? We know, of course, that Mughal emperors from the days of Akbar had claimed to possess a spiritual authority, as indeed did their Safavid contemporaries in Iran. And unlike the Safavids this authority was religiously neutral, as the Mughal emperors accepted disciples who were both Hindu and Muslim. But from being a quality attendant upon their royal power, such authority seems slowly to have become the uniquely moral virtue of a declining dynasty, one characterized by what might be termed its new constitutional role. Thus in the eighteenth century Bahadur Shah's ancestor, Shah Alam II, had also threatened to become a fakir and retire to Mecca if his Maratha protector did not send him the eyes of Ghulam Qadir, a Rohilla chieftain who had sacked Delhi and blinded the emperor.[51] Indeed the trope of the ruler as ascetic had become so common that we have already seen one of the rebel proclamations describe Queen Victoria herself as threatening to become a fakir and retire to Africa with her Ethiopian lover.

However much a part of Mughal tradition it was, we also know that this language of sacrifice was the very one that the rebels spoke, Hindus to Muslims in their case, in order to rethink at least some social relations outside the framework of India's inherited hierarchies. And in this sense Bahadur Shah was as much a product of the Mutiny as the sepoys he sought to counsel, no matter how unsuccessfully. The next such leader to emerge in India, though one far more successful, was Mahatma

Gandhi, who with his fasts unto death also put his own powerlessness on display while speaking the language of sacrifice and even promising to retire from the political arena altogether. Indeed Ahsanullah Khan's recommendation that the King should have offered his own wives and children to be put to death before countenancing the murder of others was advice that Gandhi himself uttered many times, using as his preferred example of this virtue the sacrifice of another monarch, the legendary Raja Harischandra who was willing to kill his own wife and son to fulfill his moral duty.

We might say that Queen Victoria restored the Mughal's constitutional status when she took the title Empress of India in the Mutiny's wake. In fact the Queen's Proclamation of 1858, which stopped British reprisals against the rebels and promised a policy of toleration and non-interference in India's religions, was widely seen by Indians as the new empire's founding constitution, establishing a secular order in the subcontinent that did not yet exist in the British Isles. Of course this second restoration of imperial authority presented the character of a farce when compared to the tragedy of Bahadur Shah's installation during the revolt, not least because it sought to redefine the terms of India's moral compact by robbing the Queen's subjects of all initiative in the matter. It was nevertheless the Mutiny that brought the British Empire into being, rather than the reverse, if only by ushering in the reign of tradition in all its various guises, old, new and made to order.[52] It was only with the rebellion's aftermath, in other words, that tradition came to replace modernity in the imagination of Indians and Englishmen alike.

I have been concerned in this chapter with delineating another vision of the Mutiny's modernity than the one retailed by colonial and nationalist writers. It was neither the unity of India in any political sense, nor its division in any religious one that the revolt brought to light, but rather an empire of distinctions where the native was not set against the alien but existed alongside it within a moral compact. And if much of this moral compact was drawn from tradition, I have tried to demonstrate that its hesitant achievement during the rebellion of 1857 had unexpected consequences for India's modernity. These became evident in the next period of anti-British mobilization across northern India, Gandhi's movement of non-cooperation that began with his defense of the Caliphate in 1919. The extraordinary similarity of themes and arguments between these two events must give us pause for thought, even if we do not link them in any causal fashion. Whether it is the sacrifices made by one religious group for another or the practice of non-cooperation itself, such elements appear to have been reincarnated from one historical moment to the next. For it was in the Mutiny that these factors were transformed out of traditional recognition and made into the stuff of Indian modernity, destabilizing nationalist verities even as they made the nation itself possible in Gandhi's spiritualization of politics.

2

A NATION MISPLACED

In the lengthy statement delivered during his trial for Gandhi's assassination, Nathuram Godse pointed out that the Mahatma's idea of nationality was shaped during the first two decades of his political life spent within South Africa's community of emigrant Indians. Curious about this population was the fact that it appeared to invert the demographic state of things at home, dominated as it was by the wealthy Muslim merchants for whom Gandhi worked as a lawyer. In contradiction to the state of affairs in their country of origin, these Indians were also a minority, which meant, his murderer said, that Gandhi could indeed become the leader of a unified community in which religious differences did not play a determining role. The Mahatma's fundamental mistake, however, was to insist on treating India as if it were South Africa, making what Godse saw as concession after concession to its Muslim minority so as to lead a unified nation once again, a strategy that only exacerbated religious rivalries and finally resulted in the partition of India. Gandhi, in other words, should have based his national ideal upon the interests and identity of India's religious majority in order to achieve justice for Hindus and Muslims both. The following passage conveys something of the flavour of Godse's argument:

When Gandhiji finally returned to India at the end of 1914, he brought with him a very high reputation for courageous leadership of Indians in South Africa. He had placed himself at the head of the struggle for the assertion and vindication of the national self-respect of India and for our rights of citizenship against white tyranny in that country. [...] When he returned here to serve his countrymen in their struggle for freedom, he had legitimately hoped that as in Africa he would command the unchallenged confidence and respect of all communities. But in that hope he soon found himself disappointed. India was not South Africa. In South Africa Indians had claimed nothing but the elementary rights of citizenship which were denied to them. They had all a common and acute grievance. [...] But in India communal franchise, separate electorates and the like had already undermined the solidarity of the nation, more of such were in the offing and the sinister policy of communal favouritism was being pursued by the British with the utmost tenacity without any scruple. Gandhiji therefore, found it most difficult to obtain the unquestioned leadership of the Hindus and Muslims in India as in South Africa. But he had been accustomed to be the leader of all Indians and quite frankly, he could not understand the leadership of a divided country. It was absurd for his honest mind to think of accepting the generalship of an army divided against itself.[1]

Whatever the truth or falsehood of Godse's analysis, it stands alongside the highly respectable arguments for majority-defined democracy that continue to be made into our own times. And like these arguments it is forced to recognize that even in a democracy, or indeed any other form of government in which a popular will achieves representation in ways either legal or illegitimate, political reality does not always follow the prescriptions of majority rule. For if Gandhi did not speak for the Hindu majority, then whom did his hugely successful movement represent? Godse did not evade this question by invoking notions like false consciousness or maintaining that the Mahatma simply fooled his co-religionists, and he certainly could not claim that an old man in a loincloth managed to compel a great political party like the Indian National Congress to do his bidding over several decades by political machinations alone. Gandhi's assassin was thus forced to consider very seriously the question his analysis raised: if a majority does not know its own interests, can it be said to exist at all?

Instead of proceeding in the usual fashion to describe an implicit sense of self among Hindus that had to be nudged into explicit awareness by way of propaganda, exemplary acts of sacrifice or terrorism, Godse did something almost Gandhian. He said that Hindus had set aside their interests because they trusted and revered the Mahatma, thus accepting a definition of nationality that was founded upon Muslim interests while being at the same time foreign to India. It was in order to thwart Gandhi's betrayal of the majority's faith, as well as to prevent the Mahatma himself from being betrayed by Muslims, that Godse felt obliged to kill him.[2] Apart from the curious intimacy involved in this relationship of murderer and victim, which no longer admitted of easy distinctions between friend and enemy, what is significant in Nathuram Godse's analysis is that it foregrounds the imperial or international context from which Gandhi's use of the term "Indian" emerged to define the nation, a context in which nationality was synonymous with minority not least because it was only outside India that the nation could achieve its ideal form.[3]

What Godse argued, in effect, was that the Mahatma's domination of Indian politics for an unbroken period of thirty years represented the success of a conception of nationality that was developed abroad and took for its basis a minority population, whether this was the ethnic community of Indians in South Africa or the religious community of Muslims in India. While we may demur from his interpretation of Gandhi's politics, I will argue that Godse perceived something of its nature that has since been lost to view. For the Mahatma very frequently referred to his South African experience as providing both the origins and model of the great campaigns he would go on to lead in India. Rather than constituting some obscure beginning, moreover, this experience represented the first appearance of Indian politics in an international form, one that addressed the British Empire as a whole rather than simply agitating for domestic rights in some portion of it. How then did Gandhi conceive of the Indian as an international, and by that very token a minority category?

Gandhi's empire

Unlike the conspiracies and sundry acts of terrorism that utilised foreign territories to stage an otherwise parochial form of Indian politics, the Mahatma's South African struggle was not only public and non-violent, but it also involved large numbers of people and took as its cause Indian grievances abroad. As such it could neither be confined to a law and order matter nor limited to domestic politics in India, but became instead an imperial and indeed international issue. It was this new Indian politics that made Gandhi's name, while at the same time producing a novel sense of nationality that he took back with him to India. As the Mahatma put it in *Satyagraha in South Africa*, written in 1922 to give an account of his first non-violent campaigns:

> The result of all this evidently was that the condition of Indians overseas became a question of first-rate importance in the eyes of the Imperial Government. This fact reacted for good as well as for evil in the other colonies. That is to say, in all the colonies where Indians had settled, they awoke to the importance of their own position and the Europeans awoke to the danger which they thought the Indians were to their predominance.[4]

It was not the spread of satyagraha to other parts of the empire that made Indians into political actors upon the international stage, but rather its occurrence in South Africa that offered only the promise of such expansion. In other words Indians were seen to pose a threat to the empire even if their struggles did not traverse its vast extent, because they presented a danger whose reality was always to be found elsewhere.[5] Indeed

A NATION MISPLACED

Gandhi noted that even for Englishmen and Boers in South Africa, the Indian threat loomed large not as a domestic one but precisely in the form of an imperial problem emanating from no particular place. So the Mahatma described how his very moderate speeches delivered on a visit to India had a far greater impact on public opinion in South Africa than the more radical positions he had adopted at home, to say nothing of the campaign he had led in Natal itself:

> My speeches in India were free from the slightest exaggeration. On the other hand, as I knew from experience that if we describe an event to a stranger, he sees more in it than what we intend to convey, I had deliberately described the South African situation in India less forcibly than the facts warranted. But very few Europeans would read what I wrote in Natal, and still fewer would care for it. The case, however, was obviously different with my speeches and writings in India. Thousands of Europeans would read Reuter's summaries. Moreover, a subject which is considered worthy of being communicated by cablegram becomes invested with an importance it does not intrinsically possess. The Europeans of Natal thought that my work in India carried the weight attributed to it by them and that therefore the system of indentured labour would perhaps come to an end, and hundreds of European planters would suffer in consequence. Besides, they felt blackened before India.[6]

For white men in South Africa to feel "blackened before India" meant that they, too, like the Indians for whom Gandhi spoke, viewed the problem posed by commercial and labour migration in imperial rather than national terms. But it was a curious kind of reality that this empire possessed, manifested as it was by issues like news from abroad and potential unrest that were displaced from its subjects, Indian as well as South African, in both space and time. There did exist of course a commonsense view of empire that was based upon the very real political, economic and cultural ties binding together its various parts. And it was this everyday notion that had provided the Indian National Congress with both its context and cause from the nineteenth century. For what nationalists wanted then was simply equal representation within the empire, which meant in effect dominion status like that enjoyed by Canada, Australia and other white colonies. Gandhi, however, radicalized this idea of empire to fashion a very different way of being Indian within it.

Throughout his South African career, the Mahatma claimed rights for his fellow migrants due to them neither as Indians nor South Africans but rather as citizens of the empire. He did not view this citizenship as being undifferentiated in character, expecting the Government of India to defend the particular interests of its subjects in other parts of the empire, and even acknowledging the fact that it sometimes did so. Instead of simply pushing for India to be treated like Canada, however, what Gandhi envisioned was the empire transformed into a worldwide commonwealth, whose self-governing parts would be equal and allow for the free movement of persons and products. Because it presupposed a common citizenship, this vision of the empire meant something more than a free-trade zone, constituting rather a world-historical project of freedom that for Gandhi would allow Britain to redeem herself by its accomplishment. Within such an order, majorities and minorities could only be variable categories, the same group occupying one status here and another elsewhere. For at the imperial level no majority was possible, with communities of all descriptions existing only as minorities compelled to press their claims by moral persuasion alone.

In this way, thought Gandhi, a reformed empire could become the ideal arena for a purely moral and indeed rational politics, since neither the facts of nationality nor those of demography would be able to determine popular opinion and thus political decision-making there. Like many other plans to turn the empire into a commonwealth, the Mahatma's vision was a deeply liberal one, not least because he thought that liberalism could only achieve perfection in an imperial order, where interests might appear in their naked abstraction without having to appeal to the prejudices of the greater number for success. However unlikely such a vision might seem in retrospect, there were many instances of British statesmen voicing similar sentiments in the Mahatma's time, though he considered their efforts to defend Indian rights in South Africa as insufficiently imperial. Typical, for instance, is the following comment on Britain's unwillingness or inability to pull her weight in the empire by compelling the colonies to act with justice, even as she claimed to have gone to war with the Boers at least in part to protest their treatment of Indians in the Transvaal:

> When during Lord Morley's tenure of the office of the Secretary of State for India, a deputation on behalf of the Indians waited upon him, he declared in so many words that as the members of the deputation were aware, the Imperial Government could exercise but little control over self-governing dominions. They could not dictate to them; they could plead, they could argue, they could press for the application of their principles. Indeed in some instances they could more effectively remonstrate with foreign Powers, as they remonstrated with the Boer Republic, than with their own people in the Colonies. The relations of the mother country with the colonies were in the nature of a silken tie which would snap with the slightest tension. As force was out of the question, he assured the deputation that he would do all he could by negotiations. When war was declared on the Transvaal, Lord Landsdowne, Lord Selborne and other British statesmen declared that the scandalous treatment accorded to the Indians by the South African Republic was one of the causes of the war.[7]

By this account, then, Gandhi turns out to have been a stauncher imperialist than the British themselves, his two great struggles on behalf of the empire being those that were conducted for the rights of Indians within it, and for the preservation of the Caliphate in deference to the wishes of Britain's Muslim subjects, who had contributed to the Ottoman defeat in the First World War. This latter event, which I shall look at more closely in the next chapter, represents the high water mark of Gandhian non-cooperation by its unprecedented mobilization of

THE IMPOSSIBLE INDIAN

Hindus as well as Muslims, though its international dimension has puzzled historians, who have tended to see it as an opportunistic move by which the Mahatma pandered to Muslim sentiment in order to gain their support. Yet the Khilafat Movement exhibited all the traits of Gandhi's South African campaign, dedicated as it was to a cause outside India and launched to force the empire to live up to its own ideals and transform itself into a world-encompassing liberal order.

And so just as Indians in South Africa and elsewhere in the world beyond India could, because of their status as a dispersed minority, engage with the empire as a whole, Muslims too, with their own interests and connections outside India, were capable of holding the empire accountable at its full extent. This is why India's Muslim minority served for the Mahatma as the twin of South Africa's Indian one. And so it is probably no coincidence that Gandhi penned the lengthiest account of his South African campaign during the Khilafat Movement, for which it was meant to serve as a model. But it was during this very movement that he also lost his faith in the empire, retiring thenceforth from active intervention in international affairs to focus on the Indian struggle in a more conventional fashion. And yet I will argue that the figure of the Indian as a minority with the Muslim as its twin continues to haunt nationalist politics, if only in the fears of men like Nathuram Godse, who by assassinating the Mahatma attempted to lay this spectre to rest.

Since his vision of the empire never became a reality, Gandhi had to conceive of the role that Indians played within it in rather different terms. As they were not citizens of the empire, then, he declared Indians to be its helots. This was not because their country had been colonized by Britain so much as because they provided the labourers and soldiers to secure her domains the world over, from South-East Asia to the Middle East, and from South Africa to South America. Indians could not in fact be defined by their country of origin, whose government refused to represent them, and were therefore to be identified as a people without citizenship who belonged nowhere in particular. They were a purely imperial population in a way that Englishmen, for instance, could never be. In this context it was neither India nor South Africa that provided Indians with a nationality, but satyagraha, considered as a practice without origin or destination of any territorial sort. Thus Gandhi concluded *Satyagraha in South Africa* with an acknowledgement that Indian struggles across the empire were to be defined by the practice of nonviolent resistance alone, since India could not provide them with a foundation of some political kind:

> Finally, the reader of these pages has seen that had it not been for this great struggle and for the untold sufferings which many Indians invited upon their devoted heads, the Indians today would have been hounded out of South Africa. Nay, the victory achieved by Indians in South Africa more or less served as a shield for Indian emigrants in other parts of the British Empire, who, if they are suppressed, will be suppressed thanks to the absence of Satyagraha among themselves, and to India's inability to protect them, and not because of any flaw in the weapon of Satyagraha.[8]

In this situation the struggle of a minority in South Africa could represent Indians as much as any campaign in India itself. Indeed I would go further and say that the struggles of minorities in diverse parts of the empire might serve to define what it meant to be Indian far better than anything that was possible in the mother country. And this may well account for the lively interest that nationalists at home took in the doings of their compatriots abroad, an interest that not accidentally collapsed with the end of colonial rule. Indians, after all, had only existed as a political category in the empire because India herself did not.

Tradesmen's entrance

Despite their provincial attitudes and limited educations, compared with those who led the Indian National Congress, the

Indian community in South Africa represented in many respects the kind of modernity that these Congressmen often despaired of finding in India. It was after all a group shaped entirely by capitalist relations, whether of commerce, service or labour, and had no dealings with pre-modern forms of possession or production. Similarly this was a community not violently divided by caste and religion, as Nathuram Godse had recognized, and therefore capable of achieving the kind of national character that would prove impossible in India. And finally the struggle of Indians in South Africa had to do with claiming citizenship rights in a fairly straightforward way rather than asking for safeguards or privileges on the basis of caste and religion, which was what politics in India was increasingly about and is in many respects to this day for majorities as much as minorities.

In all these ways, then, South Africa's Indians represented the national ideal and potential future of their compatriots at home, at least in the view of men like Godse, as well as those who opposed him while being at the same time devoted to a conventional idea of modern politics. But if the Indian struggle in South Africa was undeniably modern compared to the politics of racial inequality against which it was conducted, also clear is the fact that the assortment of traders, clerks and labourers who made up the Indian community can by no means be defined in the everyday terminology of modern politics. For example the traders cannot be described as a middle class, not only because they were disbarred from that category in South Africa by their race, but also because they were not even related to the Indian labourers as managers or employers. And even if some of these traders might have served them as moneylenders, the labourers were in fact economically dependent upon Boers and Englishmen, as indeed were the Sindhi merchants whom Gandhi describes in his account. In other words Indians in South Africa did not cohere as a community in any economic sense but only in a moral and political one.

A NATION MISPLACED

It was their struggle alone that linked the various parts of this Indian population together, with traders, for instance, depending upon labourers for manpower and muscle, which was how the coolie came to be the face of Gandhi's movement. This moral-political relationship was worlds removed from that of the peasant and landlord or the worker and industrialist, to say nothing of the caste and religious relations that would come to dominate nationalist politics in India. And so it was perhaps because caste did not exist as a major problem in South Africa, that the Mahatma could compare Indians there to Untouchables in the eyes of Englishmen and Boers, if only to chide his audience in the mother country for their own treatment of outcastes. Before uniting in a common struggle, Gandhi claimed, Indians had defined themselves in two ways, externally by trying to evade colonial categories seen as demeaning, and internally by relying upon sometimes highly localized distinctions. Thus in their attempts to avoid being called coolies by their colonial masters, Muslims called themselves Arabs and Zoroastrians identified as Persians, while in their internal relations Indians often identified themselves by caste and locality.[9]

What then did it mean to start calling oneself an Indian? In Gandhi's telling being Indian had nothing to do with some shared history or culture. Though he imagined that they possessed certain common characteristics such as thrift and otherworldliness, the Mahatma did not see these providing the ground for a sense of nationality among Indians. Moreover he stood against nationality conceived in carnal terms like eating together or marrying, precisely the kind of kinship-based community that Nathuram Godse favoured by advocating inter-caste dinners among Hindus. Was it because he recognized the parochialism of such a nationality that Gandhi deprecated it for one that was completely non-corporeal? When asked during the Khilafat Movement how a common nationality was possible between Hindus and Muslims when the former neither dined with nor married the latter, the Mahatma responded by criticizing such carnal notions of community as being both insufficient for and irrelevant to national unity, because he thought that distinctions of caste and community allowed Indian society to govern itself in a million different ways and thus withdraw from an unjust state. He would not therefore have these distinctions subordinated to a uniform idea of nationality that would be entirely dependent upon such a state:

> In my opinion the idea that interdining or intermarrying is necessary for national growth, is a superstition borrowed from the West. Eating is a process just as vital as the other sanitary necessities of life. And if mankind had not, much to its harm, made of eating a fetish and indulgence we would have performed the operation of eating in private even as one performs the other necessary functions of life in private. [...]. If brothers and sisters can live on the friendliest footing without ever thinking of marrying each other, I can see no difficulty in my daughter regarding every Mahomedan as a brother and *vice versa*. [...]. I should despair of ever cultivating amicable relations with the world, if I had to recognise the right or the propriety of any young man offering his hand in marriage to my daughter or to regard it as necessary for me to dine with anybody and everybody. I claim that I am living on terms of friendliness with the whole world. I have never quarreled with a single Mahomedan or Christian but for years I have taken nothing but fruit in Mahomedan or Christian households. I would most certainly decline to eat cooked food from the same plate with my son or to drink water out of a cup which his lips have touched and which has not been washed. [...]. But interdining and intermarriage have never been a bar to disunion, quarrels and worse.[10]

Not content with criticizing such a corporeal view of nationality by suggesting that its ideal of intimacy was incestuous, Gandhi went further to claim that only the absence of inter-dining and intermarriage made nationality possible as a form of mutual recognition and mutual obligation, thus doing nothing more than reactivating the political language that in the previous chapter we saw dominated the Mutiny. Indeed he went so far as to discount the carnal ties of kinship, whose supposed intimacy served as the model for another kind of nationalism, by pointing out the proscription against relations of sexuality and even commensality within the family. Given the fiction of such intimacy in family life, the Mahatma implied that any more corporeal conception of nationality would mean dispensing altogether with moral relations between people, to create a partnership among them that was based on the non-moral because unspoken and naturalized commonality of an impossible kinship:

> I hold it to be utterly impossible for Hindus and Mahomedans to intermarry and yet retain intact each other's religion. And the true beauty of Hindu-Mahomedan Unity lies in each remaining true to his own religion and yet being true to each other. [...]. What then does the Hindu-Mahomedan Unity consist in and how can it be best promoted? The answer is simple. It consists in our having a common purpose, a common goal and common sorrows.[11]

While in later years he would come to acknowledge inter-caste as well as inter-religious marriages, Gandhi's principled objection to carnal forms of collective identification did not change. Indeed his much remarked upon focus on the body and bodily practices was meant precisely to prevent such forms of collective identification, whose dark precedents may be found in the traditional rules of purity and pollution that made for caste distinction.[12] Ultimately, a common struggle alone made its participants into Indians, and in South Africa such a nationality emerged as part of an effort to guarantee the financial security of those engaged in fighting for their rights as citizens of the empire. So when the Mahatma describes the setting up of his first model community, Tolstoy Farm, he notes that it brought together a diverse set of people to live in a state of inter-dependency for the first time and thus fostered a sense of nationality among them. Yet this sense of being Indian was only the by-product of a quite different enterprise having to do with the prevention of fraud among Gandhi's friends and followers:

Till now the families of jail-going Satyagrahis were maintained by a system of monthly allowances in cash according to their need. It would not have done to grant an equal sum to all. A Satyagrahi who had a family of five persons dependent upon him could not be placed on a par with another who was a *brahmachari* without any family responsibilities. Nor was it possible to recruit only *brahmacharis* for our "army". The principle generally observed was, that each family was asked to name the minimum amount adequate to their needs and was paid accordingly on trust. There was considerable room here for fraud, of which some rogues might not fail to take advantage. Others who were honest but who were accustomed to live in a particular style naturally expected such help as would enable them to keep it up. I saw that at this rate the movement could not be conducted for any length of time. There was always the risk of injustice being done to the deserving, and undue advantage being taken by the unscrupulous. There was only one solution to this difficulty, namely, that all the families should be kept at one place and should become members of a sort of cooperative commonwealth. Thus there would be no scope for fraud, nor would there be injustice done to any. Public funds would be largely saved and the families of Satyagrahis would be trained to live a new and simple life in harmony with one another. Indians belonging to various provinces and professing divers faiths would have an opportunity of living together.[13]

The Mahatma's "cooperative commonwealth", the prototype of his future ashrams in India, therefore had a purpose more prosaic than that of creating an Indian nationality, though I would suggest that it ended up doing so by following the example of the trading castes for which Gandhi worked and of whom he was a part. For despite its reference to Tolstoy, the Mahatma's model community can be seen as a trader's society writ large. It was precisely by means of such cooperative arrangements between groups that neither dined nor married, after all, that migrant traders had settled in South Africa, arrangements that had indeed brought the future Mahatma there in the employ of Muslim merchants. Moreover the virtues of thrift and simplicity that Gandhi wanted to instantiate in Tolstoy Farm, and that he saw as peculiarly Indian traits, were in fact the very qualities by which such traders were known. Indeed the mobile sense of nationality that the Mahatma propounded, which neither required a territory for its manifestation nor even harked back to some ancestral origin, can easily be recognized in the migrant sensibility of a trading caste. Had not Gandhi himself chosen to follow the trade route from India to South Africa, not because he was compelled to do so, but because in the world of Gujarati commerce Johannesburg was closer to his home town of Porbandar than the merely geographical proximity of Calcutta?

As we have seen, traders in South Africa did not identify themselves by their country of origin but rather by caste and community, village and district. Being, as merchants, minorities by definition, they also remained unimpressed by the virtue of numbers. Moreover Gujarat, the place from which most traders in South Africa had come, lacked political integrity because it was fragmented by minor princely states while being united for administrative purposes with quite different cultural and linguistic regions to the south, as part of the Bombay Presidency. It is even possible to say that Gujarat ceased being a purely notional entity that could be exported by way of caste usage to different bits of the empire only after India's independence, once the presidency was dissolved and it became a linguistically defined state whose erstwhile principalities were soon to be suppressed. This is probably why the Mahatma's sense of nationality was so portable and by that token free from any claim to autochthony. Despite the Sanskrit ballast of so many terms in his political lexicon, then, Gandhi conceived of his practices as being universal enough to be derived from non-Indian sources. He thus took the suffering of Boer women in British concentration camps as the model for satyagraha:

When this cry of anguish reached England, the English people were deeply pained. They were full of admiration for the bravery of the Boers. The fact that such a small nationality should sustain a conflict with their worldwide empire was rankling in their minds. But when the cry of agony raised by the women in the concentration camps reached England not through themselves, not through their men, (they were fighting valiantly on the battlefield), but through a few high-minded Englishmen and women who were then in South Africa, the English people began to relent. The late Sir Henry Campbell-Bannerman read the mind of the English nation and raised his voice against the war. The late Mr. Stead publicly prayed and invited others to pray, that God might decree the English a defeat in the war. This was a wonderful sight. Real suffering bravely borne melts even a heart of stone. Such is the potency of suffering or tapas. And there lies the key to Satyagraha.[14]

The Mahatma's notion of nationality as a portable commodity carried by minorities existed, I have claimed, in an imperial context while being premised upon the culture of the trading caste. Gujarat's recent achievement of territorial as well as political integrity, however, together with the liberalization of the Indian economy, has made it into a site of investment prompting a vast migrant population to reclaim its homeland in new ways. For all these reasons Gujarat can now provide its trading castes and those for whom they serve as a model with a sense of belonging that not only tends to be chauvinistic in general but anti-Muslim in particular. Yet is it not perhaps their own former selves that these Gujaratis want to rid themselves of in the figure of the Muslim as a minority from abroad? After all Indians in South Africa had played precisely the role of such a minority for their British and Afrikaner critics. The particulars of discrimination in either case might differ but the logic of their argument remains the same.

Like Muslims in Gujarat and elsewhere in India today, Indians in South Africa were in Gandhi's time viewed as minorities who were potential majorities, their demographic status being as variable in the imperial context as the Muslim one is in a global arena. For it was not only by reason of their natural growth, however extraordinary it might be thought to be, that these minorities were feared, but also because they continue to be seen as the representatives of teeming millions abroad. Some combination of immigration, intimidation and even invasion from the world outside is thus seen as being capable of reducing a majority into a minority. Given its statistical absurdity, what does such a view entail but the fearful recognition that nation states are increasingly drawn into a world, whether imperial or global in nature, where majorities and minorities are unstable and can be reversed? What the Mahatma saw as an advantage of imperialism, namely that it could not sustain a politics of majority rule, modern-day nationalists see as a grave threat to the integrity of their countries.[15]

In Gandhi's day, however, this integrity had less to do with the country's territory than with the nature of its population. For interesting about Indian nationalism in this period was the fact that its votaries were not much concerned by borders, which they tended to describe in symbolic ways. In *Hind Swaraj*, for instance, his first programmatic text written in 1909, the Mahatma noted that the great centres of Hindu pilgrimage traced the boundaries of India, though in purely metaphysical terms.[16] Even the Hindu nationalist Savarkar referred in his book *Hindutva* to sacred rivers and the homophonous names of towns in the far north and south of India to define its frontiers in the most inexact manner.[17] The problem was not geography but population—who was to be considered an Indian? So in *Hind Swaraj*, Gandhi had to deal with the argument that India exists but Indians do not, because the coming of the Muslims and the British rendered a single nationality there impossible. In deprecating this notion the Mahatma pointed out that neither immigration nor conversion was capable of destroying a nation, and in doing so revealed that he viewed India as not dissimilar from a settler colony like South Africa, whose great political task was to accommodate different peoples.[18] And yet even the shared conditions under which most Indians lived did not suffice to make them homogenous, for one of the criticisms Gandhi levelled in the same text against the large scale mobility made possible by railways was that it made for a clash of differences.[19] The technology that brought people together, in other words, was as likely to make enemies of them as friends, which was why nationality might best be fostered by mutual ignorance. If these paradoxical utterances tell us anything, it is that neither majorities nor minorities possessed any stability in the imperial context, just as they lack it in today's global arena.

Model minorities and fearful civilizations

Instead of representing a politics of the past, then, perhaps we can recognize a glimmer of the future in Gandhi's vision of empire. It was entirely in keeping with this vision that the Mahatma focussed so single-mindedly on the minority that he almost deprived the majority of its integrity. For the minority was to Gandhi a moral category more than anything else, and he ascribed his recognition of its virtue to lessons learnt from Christian and Jewish friends in South Africa. Here is how the Mahatma describes one such lesson learnt from a friend called Symonds:

> He believed that truth is always with the minority. It was this belief of his which first drew him to me in Johannesburg, and he often humorously assured me that he would withdraw his support of me if he ever found me in a majority, as he was of opinion that truth itself is corrupted in the hands of a majority.[20]

Since a minority of this sort was open to all who wanted to join, of course, it could not be considered part of some exclusionary politics, while the majority that remained outside was incapable of playing the role of an adversary because it possessed little or no integrity of its own. Indeed Gandhi thought that only the voluntary sacrifices of a minority were capable of changing world history by the example they offered, which is why he placed, as we shall see in chapter five, such great hopes in the non-violent struggles of Jews in Nazi Germany and later of blacks in the United States. Even when the minority was violent it acted as a moral agent and so bore full responsibility for its injustice, while the equally culpable violence of the majority could only be described in the negative form of cowardice, because it required overwhelming numerical superiority to occur. This at least was the distinction Gandhi made when reflecting upon religious conflict in the last days of the Khilafat Movement, which he did by deploying the rhetoric of men like Nathuram Godse only to turn their arguments around, in claiming that Hindus could resist what he called Muslim bullying not by imitating their violence, but rather by acting as a minority in their own right:

> There is no doubt in my mind that in the majority of quarrels the Hindus come out second best. My own experience but confirms the opinion that the Mussulman as a rule is a bully, and the Hindu as a rule is a coward. I have noticed this in railway trains, on public roads, and in the quarrels which I had the privilege of settling. Need the Hindu blame the Mussulman for his cowardice? Where there are cowards there will always be bullies. They say that in Saharanpur, the Mussulmans looted houses, broke open safes and in one case a Hindu woman's modesty was outraged. Whose fault was this? Mussulmans can offer no defence for the execrable conduct, it is true. But I as a Hindu am more ashamed of Hindu cowardice than I am angry at the Mussulman bullying. Why did not the owners of the houses looted die in the attempt to defend their possessions? Where were the relatives of the outraged sister at the time of the outrage? Have they no account to render of themselves? [...] As a coward, which I was for years, I harboured violence. I began to prize non-violence only when I began to shed cowardice.[21]

As if to deter anyone who would take his characterization of Hindus and Muslims as being somehow peculiar to these communities, Gandhi went on to note that an identical relationship existed between the British and Indians of all religious persuasions, hammering home his point by saying that the "most muscular Zulus cower before English lads".[22] But though they might be bullies, the English as a minority in India and indeed the empire more generally, existed nevertheless as moral actors whose courage could only be admired. In fact the Mahatma would have no truck with a politics justified by the logic of numbers alone. So in *Hind Swaraj* Gandhi was adamant that Indians had no right to oust the British simply because they were more numerous than the former. For if all these Indians wanted to do was replace their masters then they might as well let the British continue ruling, since they had more experience in doing so than Hindus and Muslims combined. And if the British had to be removed in order to found a different kind of politics, then such nationalists should have no trouble in working alongside any Englishmen who agreed with their views.

Gandhi might also have argued that even votaries of majority rule like Godse were forced to act as minorities in order to claim moral agency for themselves. It was only as a minority prepared to sacrifice the lives of its members in order to rouse a heedless majority that the Mahatma's assassin and his companions could present themselves to the world, and in doing so to justify the very politics they sought to deny. But then by resorting to violence such men acknowledged in their own way that the majority on whose behalf they fought did not exist. Is this why they could only instantiate it by self-consciously imitating the minority whose violence they claimed to abhor? The minority problem thus turns out to be a problem of the majority instead, one that it can only resolve by taking the minority's place in a perverse fulfilment of Gandhi's recommendation. Over all these intimate struggles looms the ghost of the Indian as an imperial minority, and therefore an international subject, one come back to haunt the global arena into which India started moving with the onset of economic liberalization in the 1980s.

By the logic of Gandhi's argument, then, the majority is cowardly because it possesses no moral integrity, with its spokesmen

A NATION MISPLACED

forever worried about the collapse of the category due to internal divisions that would render it both equivalent and vulnerable to minority violence. And yet they are also drawn to the larger world in which this majority is rendered into a minority, as for instance was Godse, who after studying India's political problems reached the conclusion that Hindu numbers were important outside the context of a nation state in which they were to dominate:

> All this reading and thinking brought me to believe that above all it was my first duty to serve Hinduism and the Hindu people, as a patriot and even as a humanitarian. For, is it not true that to secure the freedom and to safeguard the just interests of some thirty crores of Hindus constituted the freedom and well-being of one fifth of the human race?[23]

We might say that the ambition as much as the fear of any majority is to become a minority, or rather to derive even its numerical significance from beyond the politics of majority rule. This indeed is the inevitable corollary of any attempt to reach out to the world, even if only with the wish to dominate it. The Mahatma had recognized the vulnerability built into this peculiar way of being a majority during his time in South Africa, when he saw it operating in the fears that both Boers and Englishmen entertained about the Indians in whom they saw a rival minority. In the imperial arena where they occurred, in other words, such threats could no longer be defined in terms of a struggle between majority and minority, but only as a competition of minorities. Yet even a numerical identity of this reduced kind was whittled away by its subordination to the metaphysical one of civilization. For this category, of such great importance to a colonial rhetoric of pedagogy and improvement, was meant precisely to forestall a politics based upon numbers, or rather upon the representation of a majority. Because their context could only be imperial, international or global, in other words, narratives of civilization displaced a politics of representation that was appropriate only for nation states, doing so by replacing the logic of numbers with moral considerations that were often meant to suppress the force of the many by the civilization of a few. Gandhi described such a moral narrative, familiar to this day in the opposition drawn between Western, democratic or humanitarian "values" against all others, in the following manner:

"South Africa is a representative of Western civilisation while India is the centre of Oriental culture. Thinkers of the present generation hold that these two civilisations cannot go together. If nations representing these rival cultures meet even in small groups, the result will only be an explosion. The West is opposed to simplicity while Orientals consider that virtue to be of primary importance. How can these opposite views be reconciled? It is not the business of statesmen, practical men as they are, to adjudicate upon their relative merits. Western civilisation may or may not be good, but Westerners wish to stick to it. They have made tireless endeavours to save that civilisation. They have shed rivers of blood for its sake. They have suffered great hardships in its cause. It is therefore too late for them now to chalk out a new path for themselves. Thus considered, the Indian question cannot be resolved into one of trade jealousy or race hatred. The problem is simply one of preserving one's own civilisation, that is of enjoying the supreme right of self-preservation and discharging the corresponding duty. Some public speakers may like to inflame the Europeans by finding fault with Indians, but political thinkers believe and say that the very qualities of Indians count for defects in South Africa. The Indians are disliked in South Africa for their simplicity, patience, perseverance, frugality and otherworldliness. Westerners are enterprising, impatient, engrossed in multiplying their material wants and in satisfying them, fond of good cheer, anxious to save physical labour and prodigal in habits. They are therefore afraid that if thousands of Orientals settled in South Africa, the Westerners must go to the wall. Westerners in South Africa are not prepared to commit suicide and their leaders will not permit them to be reduced to such straits". I believe I have impartially recapitulated the arguments urged by men of the highest character among the Europeans. I have characterised their arguments as pseudo-philosophical, but I do not thereby wish to suggest that they are groundless. From a practical point of view, that is to say, from the standpoint of immediate self-interest they have much force. But from the philosophical point of view, they are hypocrisy pure and simple. In my humble opinion, no impartial person could accept such conclusions and no reformer would place his civilisation in the position of helplessness in which those who urge these arguments have placed theirs.[24]

Whether or not it was hypocritical, as Gandhi suggested in the lengthy passage quoted above, any politics based on civilization has already taken leave of the logic of numbers that determines both minority and majority struggles. It is in this way a politics characteristic of an empire on the one hand and the globe on the other, since what is at issue in either case is the inability of majorities and minorities to operate in such spaces lacking the kind of political coherence that belongs to nation states alone. And so the Mahatma moved past this narrative of metaphysical rivalry to address its founding concept. As is well known from texts like *Hind Swaraj*, Gandhi was a stern critic of something he called modern civilization, by which he meant a form of life that belonged to no particular people but made victims of them all. In this way he pushed the notion of civilization that I have been describing to its logical conclusion by depriving it of any autochthonous character. For with the advent of modern civilization the discrepancies between its prior forms suddenly became irrelevant, so that there now existed only two civilizations, the modern and the traditional, neither of which could be identified with any particular people. In its modern incarnation, then, civilization had the uncanny ability to slip away from the grasp of those who would claim it and make of them merely the stopping points in its career. Whether it was called spirit or progress, capital or modernity, such an entity abandoned all its resting places in the end to leave them hollow shells. Modern civilization could not in other words provide a home for any nation and had to be forsaken, because it was capable of producing only the fear of loss and consequently the violence of an attempted recovery.

THE IMPOSSIBLE INDIAN

As a critic of civilization Gandhi reached the outermost limit of nationalist politics, following one trajectory taken by the idea of an Indian nation until its disintegration. For him this idea took shape within an imperial or international context, where minorities and majorities were interchangeable and India could not provide the nation with a foundation. In such a context Indians were able to possess integrity only in their persons and by way of their struggles for truth, not because they happened to resemble others who used the same name. Thus the Mahatma could claim against men like Godse that he wouldn't cease being a Hindu even if the entire community should disown him. It was this mobile and portable idea of nationality, one that I have suggested was developed from the sensibility of the migrant trader, that Gandhi set against a politics of fixed places and greater numbers. For even as he ended up encouraging a conventional project of nation-building in India by way of a common language, institutions and the like, the Mahatma in his final years was still capable of propagating a minimal but by that very token powerful conception of nationality along very different lines. When Mohammad Ali Jinnah, for example, insisted during their famous talks of 1944 that Gandhi should be proud to represent Hindus just as he represented Muslims, asking in effect the same thing of the Mahatma that his assassin would, the Muslim League's president received a now familiar response, in two parts, the first defining nationality by struggle and the second limiting it to persons instead of ideals:

The only real though awful test of our nationhood arises out of our common subjection. If you and I throw off this subjection by our combined effort, we shall be born a politically free nation out of our travail.[25]

Though I represent nobody but myself, I aspire to represent all the inhabitants of India, for I realise in my own person the misery and degradation which is their common lot irrespective of class, caste or creed.[26]

A NATION MISPLACED

With these few words Gandhi managed to reduce nationality to a negative quality, while conceiving of its representation in terms that had nothing to do with the politics of numbers. For he invoked large numbers in order to represent a magnitude of suffering, and not a factor of demography. And like Godse after him, Jinnah was unable to engage with such a position apart from calling it treacherous, hypocritical or misguided. Whether or not it was any of these things, I have tried to argue in this chapter that the Mahatma's reflections on nationality emerged within an imperial or international context, as his assassin recognized, in which minorities, majorities and homelands could not provide it any political foundation. Such a context, I would like to suggest, has been reconstituted in the shape of a global arena in our own times, one in which Gandhi's reflections have assumed a new reality, if only because they offer us another way of considering nationalist politics in a planetary context.

3

IN PRAISE OF PREJUDICE

In an essay on the German thinker Lessing, the political philosopher Hannah Arendt had occasion to remark that, "he wanted to be the friend of many men, but no man's brother".[1] By opposing the virtue of friendship to what she considered the vice of brotherhood, Arendt was pointing to the different moral worlds these two kinds of relationship occupied. For the bond of friendship entails the activity of choice, premised as it is upon distinguishing the person befriended from all others, while that of brotherhood implies an inherited commonality that enters politics only to destroy the differentiation of such choice. Brotherhood, after all, is always invoked in politics to trump all other relationships, something that is not necessarily the case with friendship, which is often conceived as a supplementary rather than exclusive relation. The point being that while friendship must recognize its condition of possibility in the world of discrimination, the condition of brotherhood can only be thought of as a unity already given in advance.

While they enter modern politics together, as models of equality between men that are no longer regulated by some paternal hierarchy, whether dominated by a king or a god, friendship and brotherhood exist at cross purposes. Indeed they represent two perhaps contradictory conceptions of egalitarian relations, those founded in choice and those based on nature. Both these conceptions are jeopardized by the presence, not to mention inclusion of women, whose formal relations with men as sexual beings might well limit if not put into question any order based on friendship or brotherhood.[2] In this chapter I will consider the way in which Gandhi elaborated a politics of friendship between Hindus and Muslims during the agitation he led for the protection of the Caliphate following Turkey's defeat in the First World War. In common with others who deploy the language of friendship or brotherhood, the Mahatma seems to have conceived of such a politics in completely masculine terms, but as we shall see no less richly for that.

Friends and family

While they have had a long religious and philosophical career, the terms friendship and brotherhood become politically imperative at a particular moment in the history of Europe, that of the emergence of liberalism out of an old paternal order. This is a moment when the unequal relationship of duty and obligation between lord and commoner, priest and parishioner, master and servant, must be subordinated to the novel sense of equality called up by nationalism and its politics of mobilization on a mass scale. If only rhetorically, this subordination is often accomplished by the promotion of some universal social bond like brotherhood, although only in a highly contradictory way.[3] Rather than acting as universal masks for the particular reality of interests, therefore, terms like friendship or brotherhood become imperative in order to overcome the political limits of a society conceived of as the totality of unequal relations.

For the purposes of this discussion I mean by liberalism the elaboration of a social order based upon the freedom of ownership and contract. It is this kind of freedom that alone makes a liberal regime of contending interests possible. For it is the freedom of ownership that determines the actions of men by the status, property or labor they might possess, exchange or acquire, all within a framework of contractual relations that makes interests what they are. Itself predicated upon the freedom of choice, however, the relationship that goes under the name of friendship differs from that of interest, if only because it cannot be defined by contract and ownership without at the same time obscuring all other interests by its rhetoric of sentiment. Unlike the common ownership of a brotherhood that is based in nature, moreover, and that can be flouted a hundred times without ceasing to remain brotherhood, the choice upon which friendship must be founded is remarkably fragile, precisely because it is has to remain disinterested to be itself.

How is friendship as an ostensibly disinterested choice to be defined within a regime of interests? I will argue that it exists there in the illiberal form of discrimination and prejudice, since friendship cannot be rationalized into an interest by the language of ownership and contractual freedom without disappearing in the process. And my object in this chapter is to describe the discrimination of friendship as it operates in one of Gandhi's boldest experiments, his attempt to rethink political relations among Indians in the colonial context of liberalism. This context was one in which the illiberal relations of Indians divided by gender, caste or religion could neither be fully destroyed, nor a set of liberal interests founded upon ownership fully developed, so that such contractual relations as existed among them came to occur only through the direct mediation of the British state.

The gradual expansion of representative government in British India, for example, was determined by constitutional provisions like separate electorates for religious communities that might have helped to shape Hindus and Muslims into distinct political interests. Mediated as it was by the state and confined to the small numbers of Indians who were qualified by their income and education to vote, however, this new politics of interest possessed a very limited institutional scope and was unable therefore to translate all the relations that existed between India's two great religious groups into its own terms. But this only meant that such everyday relations were now unhitched from the state and its institutions, and thus effectively depoliticized, since in the absence of state mediation they arose out of juxtaposition alone.[4] For once institutional politics had come to be defined by contract and interest, its links with everyday social relations were suddenly snapped, so that even when it deployed the language of friendship or brotherhood, the colonial state could only do so somewhat disingenuously and outside the logic that defined its workings.

Gandhi approached this absence of liberal politics at the everyday level by developing the prejudice that remained between Indians there into a basis for friendship. For if prejudice constitutes a relationship that is not rationalized into interest through the state and its freedom of ownership or contract, Gandhi seemed to think that it could also be made to produce friendship as the very emblem of disinterest. And this was a doubly important task, because prejudice might be the only thing that stood in the way of brotherhood as a further depoliticization of everyday life. Brotherhood, in other words, as a false unity that can only sustain itself by trivializing if not destroying the difference upon which prejudice and friendship both rely. Brotherhood, finally, as another name for hatred, since it took as its object men who must eventually betray their fraternity to a contract of interests mediated by the state. Only the desire for brotherhood, after all, makes possible the language of betrayal and revenge that was in Gandhi's time coming to mark relations among Indians, and especially Hindus and Muslims, with an increasingly ferocious violence. For by the terms of its own rhetoric such violence was premised upon a perverse desire for brotherhood with the enemy seen to have betrayed it. That the Mahatma was fully conscious of brotherhood's murderous aspect is evident from his steady identification of fraternity with fratricide, a theme to which I shall return in chapter four.

Now the colonial state in India, despite its paternalistic claims to represent the hierarchy of races or the progress of civilizations, did not employ the language of brotherhood to describe its subjects. Instead colonial rhetoric tended to stress friendship as the preferred relationship, both among Indians belonging to different religious or ethnic groups, and between them and India's foreign rulers. However, friendship was conceived within the empire not as a form of ideological universality in the way of nationalism, but rather as the essence of the particular, one that lacked the potential for national mobilization. If anything friendship was seen as a moral rather than political imperative, and one has only to think of its importance, even as an incantation in texts as diverse as Kipling's *Ballad of East and West* and Forster's *Passage to India*, to realize the seriousness of such an imperative in the colonial imagination. The imperial order might therefore be described as a form of paternalism without brotherhood, being unable to countenance any fraternal connection either between India's various peoples or between them and the British.

It is nationalism that introduces the modern language of brotherhood to Indian politics. And while Gandhi was often ambiguous about the difference between friendship and brotherhood, in light of the peculiar colonial history of these terms, I want to view him here as an advocate of the former against the latter. Gandhi, I will argue, took up the colonial idea of friendship as a moral imperative and made it productive for an anti-colonial politics. Yet just like its colonial incarnation, friendship for Gandhi was not a universal category, and certainly not one that might effect an undifferentiated national mobilization. It was instead a very particular relationship that could only subsist between certain classes of people, in this case among religious communities like Hindus and Muslims, or political classes such as the Indian and the British. Indeed the Mahatma was quite clear that friendship, or *mitrata*, was only possible among equals, while those like the so-called "Untouchables" who were placed by history or politics in a position of inferiority had to be engaged by the principle of service, or *seva*, instead.[5]

Pan-Islamic politics

The occasion for Gandhi's experiment in the prejudice of friendship was provided by the Khilafat Movement, the first manifestation of mass politics in the history of India, and one that propelled Gandhi to power in the Congress and indeed the country as a whole largely with Muslim support.[6] This extraordinary agitation began in the aftermath of the First World War as a Muslim attempt to force Britain to defend the territorial integrity of the defeated Ottoman Empire, whose sultan claimed also to be caliph, the fount of Islamic authority worldwide. The sudden and unprecedented devotion of Indian Muslims to this titular authority has never ceased to confound historical explanation, so that at most we are treated to analyses accusing the disenfranchised Muslims of India of a fantastically vicarious identification with the freedom of their co-religionists abroad, and the disenfranchised Hindus of India who joined them of an opportunistic desire to unify India for the ulterior motive of independence.

Indeed the Khilafat Movement has been seen as standing in such a contradictory relationship to Indian nationalism that its collapse in 1922 is judged to be the only outcome of an unnatural alliance. Yet the movement lasted longer than many of the Mahatma's other agitations, which for their part are not viewed as coming to an end because of some fundamental contradiction. Similarly Gandhi's introduction of Muslim divines and Islamic themes into national politics is generally regarded as a mistake, though his far more frequent engagement with specifically Hindu themes having to do with caste, conversion or cow-worship, to say nothing of his close association with Hindu religious leaders seem to raise no concerns about the encouragement of reactionary elements and fanaticism, no doubt because the latter were after all confined to India. However mistaken he might have been to espouse the cause of the Caliphate or ally himself with Muslim divines, in other words, Gandhi's actions during the movement must be seen as being of a piece with his politics more generally.

These commonplace accounts of the Khilafat Movement can be put aside when we recognize that whatever its other implications were as far as the encouragement of a religious politics among Muslims are concerned, the movement might more accurately be described as the first example of Indian nationalism's claim to speak and indeed act within the arena of international politics. Gandhi's agitation for the rights of Indians in South Africa had been a dress rehearsal of sorts for this claim, though it had been confined to demanding some measure of equality within the British Empire, and did not venture to go so far as prescribe this empire's foreign policy. On the other hand the Khilafat Movement represented an extraordinary demand, that India's role in world affairs be acknowledged even while she was a colony, thus allowing Indians to claim either the status of partners in empire, and if not then its challengers instead.

The Muslims interested in keeping at least the Islamic parts of the old Ottoman domains under Turkish rule had no intention of themselves becoming Ottoman subjects or even pledging loyalty to the Caliph. Instead they saw themselves both as British subjects asking their government to take heed of public opinion, and as Indians who wished to give their country a role in the making of a new world following the war. If anything the Khilafat Movement was an attempt not to sacrifice India's interests to the larger Islamic world so much as to make her into the leader of this world. The fantasy of India playing such a role in the world probably dates back to the end of the nineteenth century, when it was her spiritual wares that were often announced, by European as well as Indian intellectuals, as constituting the balm that might heal the travails of modernity. Perhaps the most important Indian figure to do so was Swami Vivekananda, who became the first Hindu spiritualist to appeal to the West. Given her subjection to British rule, after all, and the apparently invincible power of Europe and America, it made sense to think of India's contribution to the world as being essentially spiritual in nature, with the Mahatma himself inheriting this way of thinking.

And so there is nothing strange about Muslims thinking of their religion in the same fashion, though being a far more widely-dispersed one than Hinduism, Islam's global ambition was defined in less spiritual terms and called pan-Islamism by its enemies. But it was this definition that allowed India to make her debut on the international stage as a Muslim power, something she was not yet in a position to do in any other way. After all both Britain and her enemies, from Napoleon to Hitler, were much taken with the idea of a pan-Islamic revolt against the empire led by India's enormous population of Muslims, which happened also to be the largest in the world. When Gandhi justified the Muslim resentment at Turkey's dismemberment after her defeat in the war, he could therefore draw upon a common understanding of pan-Islamism as an element of British as much as Muslim politics, which he did when citing the following words of the Prime Minister, David Lloyd George, referring to his wartime pledge to India that the sacred sites of Islam would not be taken away from Ottoman control:

It is too often forgotten that we are the greatest Mahomedan power in the world and one-fourth of the population of the British Empire is Mahomedan. There have been no more loyal adherents to the throne and no more effective and loyal supporters of the Empire in its hour of trial. We gave a solemn pledge and they accepted it. They are disturbed by the prospect of our not abiding by it.[7]

IN PRAISE OF PREJUDICE

Only much later and indeed after her independence would factors such as socialism, anti-colonialism, non-alignment and finally nuclear capability and economic prowess permit India to play as important a role in the world as pan-Islamism did. In the meantime, since even the British Empire advertized itself as the world's greatest "Mahomedan power", the Mahatma and his associates could not be blamed for taking its claim seriously. For in doing so they were only following the lead of Indian revolutionaries more generally, whether dedicated to a Hindu revival or even communism, who like Shyamji Krishnavarma, Raja Mahendra Pratap and Har Dayal had all dallied with pan-Islamism.[8]

The empire of liberalism

Whatever the reasons were for the emergence of the Khilafat Movement, its very novelty elicited an equally original response from Gandhi, one we may explore through the speeches and articles published in his journal *Young India*. I shall begin my analysis of his arguments about Britain's "betrayal" of her Muslim subjects, then, with a description of Gandhi's views on liberalism, move on to the challenge posed by the Khilafat Movement to its regime of interests, and end with his working out of a politics of prejudice in response to this challenge. To begin with it is important to note that the Khilafat Movement, so often and contradictorily judged as nationalist or pan-Islamist in its politics, was nevertheless loyal and liberal, because it petitioned the colonial government as an association of interested subjects. This is how Gandhi described the movement's aims:

> The preservation of the Khilafat with such guarantees as may be necessary for the protection of the interests of the non-Muslim races living under Turkish rule and the Khalif's control over Arabia and the Holy Places with such arrangement as may be required for guaranteeing Arab self-rule, should the Arabs desire it.[9]

Insofar as these Levantine demands were addressed to the British government by an Indian movement, they were of course imperial demands rather than national or even pan-Islamist ones, because their terrain was that of the British Empire. But more than mere territory, this diverse empire was for Gandhi also the site where a liberal regime of interests, such as the nation with its bounded and singular identity could never be, approached universality:

> What is this British Empire? It is as much Mahomedan and Hindu as it is Christian. Its religious neutrality is not a virtue, or if it is, it is a virtue of necessity. Such a mighty Empire could not be held together on any other terms. British ministers are, therefore, bound to protect Mahomedan interests as any other.[10]

In other words the virtue of neutrality, which made the liberal arbitration of interests possible in contract, was necessary only in and as an empire where political relations could not be based on universalistic terms like brotherhood or friendship.[11] And it was because he sought to fulfill the universality of liberalism in the empire, or of the empire in liberalism, that Gandhi argued with the British on the basis of contractual interest:

> If India is to remain equal partner with every other member of the Empire, India's voting strength must be infinitely superior to that of any other member. [...] Thus, the center of equilibrium must shift to India rather than remain in England, when India has come into her own. That is my meaning of Swaraj within the Empire. [...] To-day we are striving for Swaraj within the Empire in the hope that England will in the end prove true, and for independence if she fails. But when it is incontestably proved that Britain seeks to destroy Turkey, India's only choice must be independence.[12]

Indeed Gandhi's celebrated loyalty to the empire should be taken seriously precisely because he saw in it the possibility of liberalism's universality, whose order was worthy of loyalty despite being in no sense a moral one:

IN PRAISE OF PREJUDICE

My duty to the Empire to which I owe my loyalty requires me to resist the cruel violence that has been done to the Mussalman sentiment. So far as I am aware, Mussalmans and Hindus have as a whole lost faith in British justice and honor. [...] In these circumstances, the only course open to one like me is either in despair to sever all connection with British rule, or, if I still retained faith in the inherent superiority of the British constitution to all others presently in vogue, to adopt such means as will rectify the wrong done, and thus restore confidence. I have not lost faith in such superiority and am not without hope that somehow or other justice will yet be rendered. [...] Indeed, my conception of that constitution is that it helps only those who are ready to help themselves. I do not believe that it protects the weak. It gives free scope to the strong to maintain their strength and develop it. The weak under it go to the wall.[13]

Now defending an empire in which one's own country is to dominate may be disingenuous, if not hypocritical, but it is exactly prejudice of this sort, after all, that belongs at the heart of liberalism as interest. Prejudice then does not pose a problem in its own right, but only when it is not translated into an interest to be managed contractually. For without such a translation prejudice invariably exceeds the regime of interests to set its limits. These limits to a liberal order might or might not be exceptional, but they are certainly produced by this order itself in a logic whose end is often violent. Thus Gandhi describes the violence of one possible outcome in the dismemberment of the Ottoman Empire, the setting aside of some part of it for a Jewish homeland, as if it followed naturally from a liberalism that constituted interests in such a way that once disconnected from the arbitration of the state, they could only turn to mutual strife:

Britain has made promises to the Zionists. [...] The Jews, it is contended, must remain a homeless wandering race unless they have obtained possession of Palestine. I do not propose to examine the soundness or otherwise of the doctrine underlying the proposition. All I contend is that they cannot possess Palestine through a trick or a moral breach. Palestine was not a stake in the war. The British Government could not dare have asked a single Muslim soldier to wrest control of Palestine from fellow-Muslims and give it to the Jews. Palestine, as a place of Jewish worship, is a sentiment to be respected, and the Jews would have a just cause of complaint against Musulman idealists if they were to prevent Jews from offering worship as freely as themselves. [...] By no canon of ethics or war, therefore, can Palestine be given to the Jews as a result of the war. Either Zionists must revise their ideal about Palestine, or, if Judaism permits the arbitrament of war, engage in a 'holy war' with the Muslims of the world with the Christians throwing in their influence on their side.[14]

If Gandhi argued with the British not only on their terms, but also for their terms, he did so with a realization of the limits of these terms. And faced with what he saw as British recalcitrance, it was to these limits that Gandhi turned when arguing with Indians for a cause whose pan-Islamic reach allowed him to espouse for the first time an issue beyond the particularity of their interests:

The Khilafat question has now become a question of questions. It has become an imperial question of the first magnitude.[15]

Indeed Gandhi was adamant about the importance of this issue international enough to grapple with the empire in its entirety, refusing even to compare it to something as local as the British massacre of civilians at Jallianwala Bagh in 1919. This latter event, after all, did not arise out of the terms of the Treaty of Versailles, and so could not legitimately be linked to its formulation of a new political order for the world. Only the Khilafat Movement, and by extension Islam, raised Indian concerns to imperial or international heights because it had political implications that extended beyond the would-be borders of a national state. Here is one way in which Gandhi transformed colonial and nationalist anxieties about pan-Islamism into a productive if still ambivalent political idea:

However grievous the wrong done in the Punjab, it is after all a domestic affair and it would show on our part a want of sense of proportion to bring in the Punjab grievances to justify our non-co-operation in the Imperial celebration. The Punjab grievance does not arise out of the peace terms as does the Khilafat question. We must isolate the Khilafat question if we wish to give it its proper place and value. In my humble opinion, it is not open to us to refuse to share the peace celebrations on grounds other than those that arise directly out of the peace and that touch the vital parts of our national existence. The Khilafat question alone satisfies these two tests.[16]

Pan-Islamism seems to have provided Gandhi with something like an alternative model to the British Empire. Even in his earliest book, *Hind Swaraj*, the Mahatma had reconstituted the geography of the empire by his very use of the Arabic word *Hind*, which had become archaic both in Gujarati and English, to designate an India not of the past but the future. *Hind*, of course, also existed in an imaginative geography that belied the official territoriality of the British Empire, suggesting instead the more amorphous spaces of a Muslim geographical imagination. *Hind*, after all, could not exist on the same map as the Aden Protectorate or the Dominion of South Africa, but only within the cartography of generally extinct and in any case non-political places. All this is completely unsurprising given Gandhi's own curious navigation of Britain's imperial space as if he were using an astrolabe from older imaginings of the area. But as the following statement from the introduction to a collection of the Mahatma's speeches and writings illustrates, there was nothing old-fashioned about the geopolitical alternative to imperialism that the Khilafat agitation might make possible:

It is only a people whose mentality has been perverted that can soothe itself with the domination by one race from a distant country, as a preventative against the aggression of another, a permanent and natural neighbor. Instead of developing strength to protect ourselves against those near whom we are permanently placed, a feeling of incurable impotence has been generated. Two strong and brave nations can live side by side, strengthening each other through enforcing constant vigilance, and maintain in full vigor each its own national strength, unity, patriotism and resources. If a nation wishes to be respected by its neighbors it has to develop and enter into honorable treaties. These are the only natural conditions of national liberty; but not a surrender to distant military powers to save oneself from one's neighbors. [...] The Indian struggle for the freedom of Islam has brought about a more lasting *entente* and a more binding treaty between the people of India and the people of the Mussalman states around it than all the ententes and treaties among the Governments of Europe. No wars of aggression are possible where the common people on the two sides have become grateful friends. The faith of the Mussulman is a better sanction than the seal of the European Diplomats and plenipotentiaries. Not only has this great friendship between India and the Mussulman States around it removed for all time the fear of Mussulman aggression from outside, but it has erected round India a solid wall of defense against all aggression from beyond, against all greed from Europe, Russia or elsewhere. No secret diplomacy could establish a better *entente* or a stronger federation than what this open and non-governmental treaty between Islam and India has established. The Indian support of the Khilafat has, as if by a magic wand, converted what was once the Pan-Islamic terror for Europe into a solid wall of friendship and defense for India.[17]

India, in other words, could only play her destined role in the world by making herself at home in and drawing strength from the geopolitical neighborhood in which she was permanently placed. And this meant freeing herself from the fear that attached her to the interested protection of a distant power and, in the days before anti-colonialism, communism or non-alignment had become real political options on the international stage, to attain greatness by way of an alliance between Islam and Hinduism.

Idealism abroad

But more was at stake in the international character of the Khilafat Movement than some antiquated geographical imaginary that I am for the purposes of this chapter calling Muslim. For the Khilafat Movement was not international because of the extent of its constituency so much as because it revealed itself in a millennial struggle between Christianity and Islam:

IN PRAISE OF PREJUDICE

The Great Prelates of England and the Mahomedan leaders combined have brought the question to the fore. The Prelates threw down the challenge. The Muslim leaders have taken it up.[18]

Gandhi seemed to suggest that whatever the interests were of the parties concerned, the dismemberment of the Ottoman Empire could only play itself out as a conflict of prejudices outside the bounds of state arbitration, and despite the efforts of the League of Nations to reinstate a forum for such arbitration following the collapse of the Concert of Europe:

Oppose all Turkish misrule by all means, but it is wicked to seek to efface the Turk and with him Islam from Europe under the false plea of Turkish misrule. [...] Was the late war a crusade against Islam, in which the Mussalmans of India were invited to join?[19]

I do say that the affront such as has been put upon Islam cannot be repeated for a century. Islam must rise now or 'be fallen' if not for ever, certainly for a century.[20]

Indian Muslims, therefore, were engaged in an imperial or international struggle that could not be appropriated or translated by the state into any contractual interest, but had to manifest itself in a novel way as a religious ideal:

In my opinion, if the demands of the Muslims of India are conceded, it will not much matter whether Turkey's are satisfied or not. And this for two reasons. The Khilafat is an ideal and when a man works for an ideal, he becomes irresistible. The Muslims, who represent the ideal, have behind them the opinion of the whole mass of the Indian people.[21]

What I venture to commend to [...] Christians [...] is to join the defense of the Khilafat as an ideal, and thus recognize that the struggle of Non-co-operation is one of religion against irreligion.[22]

It was on the basis of this prejudice in the form of religion, then, that Gandhi tried to make of the Khilafat Movement a refutation of that politics of interest characterizing the Peace of Versailles:

If India—both Hindu and Mahomedan—can act as one man and withdraw her partnership in this crime against humanity which the peace terms represent, she will soon secure a revision of the treaty and give herself and the Empire at least, if not the world, a lasting peace.[23]

The age of misunderstanding and mutual warfare among religions is gone. If India has a mission of its own to the world, it is to establish the unity and the truth of all religions. This unity is established by mutual help and understanding between the various religions. It has come as a rare privilege to the Hindus in the fulfillment of this mission of India to stand up in defense of Islam against the onslaught of the earth-greed of the military powers of the West. [...] If Hindus and Mussalmans attain the height of courage and sacrifice that is needed for this battle on behalf of Islam against the greed of the West, a victory will be won not alone for Islam, but for Christianity itself. Militarism has robbed the crucified God of his name and his very cross and the World has been mistaking it to be Christianity. After the battle of Islam is won, Islam and Hinduism together can emancipate Christianity itself from the lust for power and wealth which have strangled it now, and the true Christianity of the Gospels will be established. This battle of non-cooperation with its suffering and peaceful withdrawal of service will once and for all establish its superiority over the power of brute force and unlimited slaughter. What a glorious privilege it is to play our part in this history of the world, when Hinduism and Islam will unite on behalf of Christianity, and in that strife of mutual love and support each religion will attain its own truest shape and beauty.[24]

The idealism of the Khilafatist cause provided Gandhi with a position from which to focus on the everydayness of Indian relations in general, and in order to develop them politically. He did this first by insisting upon the irreducibility of prejudices, which could not be negotiated into interests amenable to a reason that is always a reason of state. Thus his description of the Muslim claim:

If the Muslim claim was unjust apart from the Muslim scriptures, one might hesitate to support it merely on scriptural authority. But when a just claim is supported by scriptures, it becomes irresistible.[25]

I cannot regulate the Mahomedan feeling. I must accept his statement that the Khilafat is with him a religious question in the sense that it binds him to reach the goal even at the cost of his own life.[26]

IN PRAISE OF PREJUDICE

Without a calculus of interests, of course, conventional politics becomes impossible, and so even the famous pledge to Muslims regarding the preservation of the Ottoman Empire, which the British Prime Minister was supposed to have broken, can be spoken of not as a breach of contract but a violation of prejudice in the form of sentiment:

[T]he people must not be party to a wrong-a broken pledge-a violation of deep religious sentiment.[27]

In my opinion Hindu India is solidly on your side, for your cause is not merely scripturally true, but it is morally just, and presently England will be on our side when [...] Englishmen learn that *British honour is at stake* [...].[28]

Perhaps Gandhi's most spectacular avowal of prejudice, however, and so also his denial of that whole mutuality of compromise characteristic of liberal contract, came with his refusal to make Hindu participation in the Khilafat Movement conditional, whether upon Muslim support for Indian political reforms, or indeed upon Muslim abstention from cow slaughter. Cow slaughter itself, of course, was like the Khilafat an issue seemingly intractable to the rationality of liberal interests, precisely a prejudice of the sort that liberal Hindus found embarrassing:

I trust that the Hindus will realize that the Khilafat question overshadows the Reforms and everything else.[29]

The test of friendship is assistance in adversity, and that too, unconditional assistance. Co-operation that needs consideration is a commercial contract and not friendship. Conditional co-operation is like adulterated cement which does not bind. It is the duty of the Hindus, if they see the justice of the Mahomedan cause, to render co-operation. If the Mahomedans feel themselves bound in honour to spare the Hindus' feelings and to stop cow-killing, they may do so, no matter whether the Hindus co-operate with them or no. Though, therefore, I yield to no Hindu in my worship of the cow, I do not want to make the stopping of cow-killing a condition precedent to co-operation. Unconditional co-operation means the protection of the cow.[30]

This last sentence, which makes the protection of the cow audaciously depend upon the lack of agreement between Hindus and Muslims, negates even a relationship among Indians that is based on the implicit contract of recognition. For what structures a friendship founded upon prejudice is not the abstract recognition of Hindus as Hindus and of Muslims as Muslims, but rather an everyday neighborliness, whose particularistic contiguity overrides all the implicitly universal rights of liberal recognition:

> I am sorry to have to confess that the ordinary Mahomedan entertains today no affection for Englishmen. He considers, not without some cause, that they have not played the game. But if I am friendly towards Englishmen, I am no less so towards my countrymen, the Mahomedans. And as such they have a greater claim upon my attention than Englishmen.[31]

> I have already stated that, if I were not interested in the Indian Mahomedans, I would not interest myself in the welfare of the Turks any more than I am in that of the Austrians or the Poles. But I am bound as an Indian to share the sufferings and trials of fellow-Indians.[32]

Now neighborliness, while it does imply some form of proximity, by no means presupposes a place, however constituted, as its arena of occurrence. Indeed the duties of neighborliness extend outside any place, so that even a threat to the neighborhood itself can be contemplated with understanding, if also with regret:

> Let Hindus not be frightened by Pan-Islamism. It is not—it need not be—anti-Indian or anti-Hindu. Mussalmans must wish well to every Mussalman state, and even assist any such state, if it is undeservedly in peril. And Hindus, if they are true friends of Mussalmans, cannot but share the latter's feelings. We must, therefore, co-operate with our Mussalman brethren in their attempt to save the Turkish Empire in Europe from extinction.[33]

> The Mahomedan speakers gave the fullest and frankest assurances that they would fight to a man any invader who wanted to conquer India, but they were equally frank in asserting that any invasion from without undertaken with a view to uphold the prestige of Islam and to vindicate justice would have their full sympathy if not their actual support. It is easy enough to understand and justify the Hindu caution. It is difficult to resist the Mahomedan position.[34]

IN PRAISE OF PREJUDICE

The fact that Gandhi refuses to posit some third entity like the state as a neutral arbiter making possible the contract of interests means that he does not recognize the need for any arbitration apart from the relation of neighborliness itself. Now it is the state that generally provides a neutral ground for the establishment of contractual relations between interests, and it represents therefore the kind of universality that we have seen reaches its consummation in liberalism. As a ground for such relations, the universal mediation of the state constitutes an origin as much as institutional site, one that literally produces a fraternity of subjects. In defying its mediation, therefore, Gandhi also rejected the kind of narratives that both united people in, and divided them by, lines of political descent and causality that had their origins in the state. Thus he refused to accept responsibility even for the consequences of his own actions, instead manufacturing an independence from such origins out of sheer irresponsibility:

> It is perfectly true that I am assisting and countenancing the union between Hindus and Moslems, but certainly not with "a view of embarrassing England and the Allied Powers in the matter of the dismemberment of the Ottoman Empire". It is contrary to my creed to embarrass Governments or anybody else. This does not however mean that certain acts of mine may not result in embarrassment. But I should not hold myself responsible for having caused embarrassment when I resist the wrong of a wrongdoer by refusing assistance in his wrong-doing.[35]

> But I must refuse to be deterred from a clear course, because it may be attended by violence totally unintended and in spite of extraordinary efforts that are being made to prevent it. At the same time I must make my position clear. Nothing can possibly prevent a Satyagrahi from doing his duty because of the frown of the authorities. I would risk, if necessary, a million lives so long as they are voluntary sufferers and are innocent, spotless victims.[36]

It is easy, and even profitable, to read Gandhi's irresponsibility in the celebrated terms of the Danish philosopher Søren Kierkegaard's essay *Fear and Trembling*, according to which the realm of ethics actually denies individual responsibility by its very universality.[37] In other words the universally communicable claims of this ethical realm create communities of moral sentiment that rob the responsible act of its interiority, and so of its absolute character as well.[38] All of which means that only an irresponsible act, such as Abraham's willingness to sacrifice his son without reference to the ethical universality of any divine commandment, implies the existence of absolute responsibility.[39] However apt the comparison with Kierkegaard, his aristocratic morality sits uneasily alongside Gandhi's concern with those elements of everyday life that also escape universality. One way we can understand these elements is by looking at what Gandhi is willing to bear responsibility for. In the passage quoted above, for example, he refuses to take responsibility for any violence that might result from the lack of mass discipline in non-cooperation, but claims complete responsibility for the violent deaths of up to a million disciplined people.

Two years later, in 1922, the Mahatma called off his most successful experiment in non-cooperation, much to the chagrin of his allies, because of the mass violence committed by his followers at Chauri-Chaura, for which he held himself completely accountable.[40] This action, which effectively ended the Khilafat Movement, illustrates something more than Gandhi's mistrustful or paternalistic attitude towards mass politics. It demonstrates perhaps the Mahatma's attempt to become a political agent by laying claim to his very lack of agency, if this is defined as the control and ownership of an act in such a way that a subject becomes responsible only for what he possesses. Indeed Gandhi performed penances throughout his career to expiate for instances of violence which he had not himself committed, in this way overturning the contractual nature of all relations founded on juridical ideas of responsibility. Gandhi's claims to responsibility, rather, bore the mark of prejudice as friendship, for he claimed responsibility and did penance for another's acts rather than his own.

IN PRAISE OF PREJUDICE

Uncommon morality

In his effort to develop the inevitability of prejudice into a friendship that was distinct from brotherhood, Gandhi also emphasized the differences between friends, and this to such a degree that it became impossible to identify the causes that brought them together with shared affections, as one would in an ideology of brotherhood for instance. Thus the Mahatma scrupulously distinguished his own affections from those of the Muslim advocates of non-cooperation:

> I can think out plans but execution must ever rest with Mussalman workers. The movement must be worked and led by them with the assistance of friends like me but also without, if need be. I must not be expected to make Non-co-operators; Mussalman leaders alone can make them. No amount of sacrifice on my part will produce in the Mussalman world the spirit of Non-co-operation, *i.e.*, sacrifice in a matter of religion.[41]

Indeed his dislike of commonality even prompted Gandhi to abandon the notion of political representation as suggesting some false and therefore potentially violent identification with a fraternity. Thus his celebrated refusal from 1940 to become even a four-*anna* member of the Indian National Congress, and thus his infuriating refusal to negotiate either with the British, or indeed with the Muslim League, as an authorized representative of this Congress. During the Khilafat Movement the Mahatma went out of his way to deny both his own representative character and that of his Muslim associates as well, thus forcing Indians to support them on moral grounds that had little to do with any sense of collective identification:

> But I do not pretend to represent Mussalman opinion. I can only try to interpret it. I could not stand alone and expect to carry the Mussalman masses with me.[42]

> This Committee [...] has the least representative capacity. Shaukat Ali is an amiable man but a rabid fanatic carrying no weight with anybody, Hasrat Mohani a useless man who thinks of nothing but Swadeshi, Dr. Kitch-

lew a man of yesterday with no experience of the world outside Amritsar. Much the same may be said against the others. I am no doubt a superior person but after all a crank and an interloper at that. Any representation signed by it will carry little weight with the outside world in so as far as it depends upon the influence of the signatories.[43]

But the discriminating friendship that one Indian might entertain for another was not dictated by the unpredictability of affection. For one thing, Gandhi required of these Indians a certain investment in the ideal of friendship, investment he thought could be made in suffering alone. This suffering, however, was motivated neither by the compassion that is as unpredictable as affection, nor by the endurance of some common privation. It consisted rather in the deliberate choice of an experience whose independence both invited and sustained friendship:

Both the Mussalmans and the Hindus are on their trial. Is the humiliation of the Khilafat a matter of concern to the former? And if it is, are they prepared to exercise restraint, religiously refrain from violence and practice Non-co-operation without counting the material loss it may entail upon the community? Do the Hindus honestly feel for their Mahomedan brethren to the extent of sharing their sufferings to the fullest extent? The answer to these questions, and not the peace terms, will finally decide the fate of the Khilafat.[44]

And to-day if I have thrown in my lot with the Mahomedans a large number of whom bear no friendly feelings towards the British, I have done so frankly as a friend of the British and with the object of gaining justice and of thereby showing the capacity of the British constitution to respond to every honest determination when it is coupled with suffering.[45]

The idealism of the Khilafat Movement, in other words, was to be sustained by a personal investment in suffering which invited rather than gave friendship. The exquisite courtesy of such a relationship resided in the fact that it made one party available to another as a friend without either an offering or a taking, which, even if unconditional, could only form the mirror-image of contract as a mode of exchange. The solitary form of suffering that Gandhi recommended, moreover, radicalized the kind of collective sensibility that is made possible by some shared experience, one that is generally said to unify its subjects unthinkingly and as if by default. For what the Mahatma's carefully chosen forms of suffering did was to reproduce this kind of sensibility by an act of will, in a way that separated the individual's experience from any collective history. That is to say Gandhi's conversion of suffering into a choice freely made by the individual ended up setting aside its historical memory as a form of collective experience that made brotherly obligation possible. In making friendship available on the uncommon ground of solitary experience, then, suffering operated prejudicially, indeed even by brinkmanship, as when the spectacle of Gandhi's own suffering in the form of fasts voluntarily undertaken so often forced rivals to parley. Thus suffering in this sense made for a friendship that was neither affection nor agreement, but perhaps a relationship of desires that diverged and were even opposed, and that yet desired one another. What this might mean we can see in Gandhi's accounting for the friendship of Hindus and Muslims in the Khilafat Movement. This is what he has to say, for example, about the Muslim reasons for such a friendship:

I do not know that I have a right to arrogate greater purity for myself than for our Mussalman brethren. But I do admit that they do not believe in my doctrine of non-violence to the full extent. For them it is a weapon of the weak, an expedient. They consider Non-co-operation without violence to be the only thing open to them in the war of direct action. I know that, if some of them could offer successful violence, they would do to-day. But they are convinced that, humanly speaking, it is an impossibility. For them, therefore, Non-co-operation is a matter not merely of duty but also of revenge. [...] Although therefore their view-point is different from mine, I do not hesitate to associate with them and invite them to give my method a trial, for, I believe that the use of a pure weapon even from a mistaken motive does not fail to produce some good, even as the telling of truth, if only because for the time being it is the best policy, is at least so much to the good.[46]

And here are what Gandhi deems to be the Hindu reasons for offering Muslims their friendship:

But I would not go with the Mussalmans in any campaign of violence. I could not help them in promoting, for instance, an invasion of India through Afghanistan or otherwise for the purpose of forcing better peace terms. It is, I hold, the duty of every Hindu to resist any inroad on India even for the purpose specified as it is his duty to help his Mussalman brethren to satisfy their just demands by means of Non-co-operation or other form of suffering, no matter how great, so long as it does not involve loss of India's liberty or inflicting violence on any person. And I have thrown myself whole-heartedly into the Non-co-operation movement if only because I want to prevent any such armed conflict.[47]

These thoroughly prejudiced accounts, of accounts equally prejudiced, reveal for Gandhi a friendship that is interested but is not an interest. For this friendship involves no *quid pro quo*, only a desire for the friend in both senses of the phrase, that is to say a desire that the friend should be such and such, and that he should do such and such. And it is in this 'desire for', removed from the already fulfilled and so extinct desire of both contractual and brotherly agreement, where Gandhi seems finally to place friendship:

My goal is friendship with the world, and I can combine the greatest love with the greatest opposition to wrong.[48]

Now Gandhi can and indeed has been accused of promoting his particular brand of friendship only to preserve the privileges of a specifically Hindu discrimination in all relations of caste and religion.[49] Such as it is, however, this discrimination is argued coherently enough to leave no hypocritical gap between prejudice and friendship, so that the Mahatma's discourse only becomes false when he falls, as he does now and then, into the language of interest or brotherhood. Of these lapses, the former is less offensive, since we have already seen that interest received Gandhi's assent in the form of a liberalism that friendship might oppose but cannot displace. And so it is only to be expected that for the Mahatma the relationship between interest and friendship is oppositional and indeed prejudiced, existing as it does without the universalizing possibility of mediation.

Brotherhood of the egalitarian or nationalist sort, however, remained to be thought through by Gandhi, for if it is not simply to be accepted as universally given, such a fraternity can only be understood posthumously, as having been betrayed by a particular interest, thus becoming in fact an impossibility. But then this was not the only language of brotherhood available to the Mahatma. Still possible even today is the old hierarchical notion of brotherhood, in whose terms the Muslim is defined as the Hindu's younger brother (and so also his sexual rival), a notion that is set up for a rhetoric of betrayal and violence, complete with evocations of the division of a paternal inheritance. This inheritance, India, was nevertheless imagined as the mother of both Hindus and Muslims by Gandhi as by other nationalists. So the Mahatma's repeated descriptions of the partition of India as the vivisection of a mother by her sons represents an interesting reversal of the Solomonic parable, for which it is the son who is to be partitioned between two mothers.

Another idea of brotherhood that Gandhi frequently used, however, was a specifically Gujarati one, in which language the term brother (*bhai*) and indeed sister (*ben*) are routinely appended to all proper names, whether of relatives or strangers. Brotherhood here works in a nominal way, with no naturalist or even nationalist connotations attached. The Mahatma himself made this clear in a letter to an American couple who had become vegetarians and taken the names Govindbhai and Radhabehn, pointing out that "[a]ccording to Indian custom, between friends 'Radha behn' is mere 'Radha'. The omission of the suffix *behn*, meaning sister, is a mark of great endearment and intimacy. If you were writing to a casual acquaintance or an utter stranger, then you will naturally mention 'Radha' by her full name 'Radhabehn'. Therefore, I dare not call you 'Govindbhai' and 'Radha' as 'Radhabehn'. *Bhai* means brother, but when *behn* and *bhai* are used as suffixes to a name, they have merely an honorific value".[50]

Perhaps it was because Gandhi faced a choice between the violence of national brotherhood and that of liberal interest that he felt compelled to speak of friendship as something irreducible to either. Friendship, indeed, as a relationship that did not merely align itself along given boundaries, like those dividing Hindus and Muslims, but that found itself inside such boundaries as well. Apart from the primacy of neighborliness, therefore, Gandhi did not differentiate between various kinds of friendship:

> My personal religion however allows me to serve my countrymen without hurting Englishmen or for that matter anybody else. What I am not prepared to do to my blood-brother I would not do to an Englishman. I would withdraw co-operation from him if it became necessary, as I had withdrawn from my own brother (now deceased) when it became necessary. I serve the Empire by refusing to partake in its wrong.[51]

I have cited this text not to illustrate Gandhi's even-handedness so much as to point out that his translation of fraternal givenness into the politics of friendship introduces rather than dissipates antagonism in such a relation. For if friendship is not given in advance, if it is always to be worked out, then a friend is a friend because potentially always a stranger, if not an enemy. In fact it might well be the latter possibility, of enmity, that finally gives friendship meaning. In other words friendship should be seen not as an effort to pre-empt enmity, but instead enmity recognized as friendship's very condition of possibility. After all, moral life in general can only reveal itself in the face of enmity. This might be why the fraught relationship between Hindus and Muslims became for Gandhi exemplary of all moral relations. Whatever the reasons, then, for the rise and fall of the Khilafat Movement, it did provide Gandhi with his boldest experiment in what we might call the politics of prejudice.

4

BROTHERS IN ARMS

The story has often been told of Gandhi putting an end to the first and arguably most successful experiment with non-cooperation across India in 1922, after some of his followers burnt to death nineteen policemen trapped in their station at a place called Chauri-Chaura. Explanations of why the Mahatma should have called off a movement that was enjoying an extraordinary success include, on the one hand, his fear of losing control over its potentially revolutionary drift, and on the other his realization that the Indians who took to all manner of violence during the satyagraha were not quite ready for their freedom. I am interested neither in the communist theory of Gandhi as an agent of some bourgeois nationalism desperate to rein in the people's revolutionary impetus, nor, for its part, in the liberal theory of a people too immature for independence. Such explanations cannot account for awkward details like the fact that no situation could be very revolutionary that was stopped by a man to whom no police or military force was available, or the fact that Gandhi had consistently demanded immediate self-rule and always rejected the claim of India's being unprepared for independence.[1]

Nonviolent protest was for the Mahatma not a means but an end in itself, one that stood apart from politics conceived as a practice of conjuring up some future. While such forms of civil disobedience had political consequences, in other words, their purposes were achieved in the very moment of expression rather than subsequently. And so acts of nonviolent resistance were already free and did not require an independent or democratic state for their guarantee. Indeed it was only this kind of freedom that deserved the name, being immediately within the reach of anyone who desired it, no matter how powerless or oppressed. When Gandhi's would-be followers resorted to violence in 1922, therefore, they had already lost their freedom, not by abandoning morality so much as by forsaking the immediate virtues of satyagraha for a politics dedicated to some time other than the present, whether this was in order to avenge a past or create a future. In fixing upon the present as a site of freedom Gandhi refused any politics that would sacrifice it for the future, and indeed inverted this logic to say that only by sacrificing the future can we safeguard it. For a future known ahead of time would no longer be true to itself, while at the same time blinding us to the possibility of incalculable change, which the Mahatma identified with the working of God in history. So in his 1924 preface to *Satyagraha in South Africa*, Gandhi described moral action in the present as a *dharma yuddha* or holy war, because it risked everything to attend upon and welcome the incalculable:

That is the beauty of Satyagraha, it comes up to oneself; one has not to go out in search for it. This is a virtue inherent in the principle itself. A dharma-yuddha, in which there are no secrets to be guarded, no scope for cunning and no place for untruth, comes unsought; and a man of religion is ever ready for it. A struggle which has to be previously planned is not a righteous struggle. In a righteous struggle God Himself plans campaigns and conducts battles. A dharma-yuddha can be waged only in the name of God, and it is only when the Satyagrahi feels quite helpless, is apparently on his last legs and finds utter darkness all around him, that God comes to the rescue.[2]

BROTHERS IN ARMS

The Mahatma sought to inhabit the present in such a way as to maintain both its own integrity and that of a moral life possible in no other time. Thus his promises made throughout a lengthy career that self-rule might be achieved within a year, or his calls for the British to depart India immediately and let her suffer invasion or civil war, as in the famous Quit India Movement of 1942 to which I shall return in chapter six. Like the Mahatma's often voiced intention of living until the age of a hundred and twenty-five, an aim he forsook after the partition of India, these statements treated the future not as an end to be achieved politically but rather as a truth already given in the present. Indeed the effort required to make such a future possible had nothing to do with influencing events or persons in a world outside one's reach, but resided instead in practices of nonviolence and non-cooperation that were in the control of any individual. It is because they were practices of self-purification that such efforts to create a future could be so certain while at the same time completely lacking instrumentality.[3] The philosopher Mohammad Iqbal had perhaps the most acute comment to make about Gandhi's focus on the present in a speech delivered to the All-India Muslim Conference in March of 1932. He claimed that the struggle of imperialism and nationalism in India was based upon a fundamental misunderstanding. For oriented as they were to the future in which their ideals lay, the British were unable to recognize themselves as oppressors in the present, while Gandhi was equally unable to grasp that his interlocutors could only be engaged by arguments that invoked this future:

The Western man's mental texture is chronological in character. He lives and moves and has his being in time. The Eastern man's world-consciousness is non-historical. To the Western man things gradually become; they have a past, present and future. To the Eastern man they are immediately rounded off, timeless, purely present [...]. The British as a Western people cannot but conceive political reform in India as a systematic process of gradual evolution. Mahatma Gandhi as an Eastern man sees in this attitude nothing more than an ill-conceived unwillingness to part with power and tries all sorts of destructive negations to achieve immediate attainment. Both are elementally incapable of understanding each other. The result is the appearance of a revolt.[4]

Whether or not Gandhi's struggles missed their mark, he well understood that the future was his enemy's greatest redoubt. Not only the mental texture of Western man, but modern politics itself was founded upon predicting and controlling the future, which was why the Mahatma set out to oppose it in a venture he called a holy war, whose battles were about setting moral action in the present against a politics of the future. I am not claiming that Gandhi was not a politician and never planned for the future, only that his commentary on the *Bhagavad-Gita* that forms the subject of this chapter, like some of his own acts, might be considered experiments in morality as a strictly contemporary practice. My task is therefore to describe the way in which Gandhi thought about such action after the failure of his first great satyagraha in 1922. Not the explanation of an event, then, but rather the words and actions of Gandhi as he struggled to come to terms with what he called "the death of non-violence" are significant, since they provide us with an exemplary analysis of moral life in the shadow of modern politics. That the Mahatma took responsibility for the failure of his nonviolent form of civil disobedience indicates that he thought it to be one of theory rather than practice. What he learnt from this failure was to attend to the nature of violence more closely, as something embodied not simply in crimes like arson or murder, but more generally as a quality inherent in all action. Violence occupied Gandhi not as a political, let alone a peculiarly Indian problem, but as a problem of everyday life. Yet it was the battlefield that provided him with a site to think about such violence, specifically the battlefield of the *Bhagavad-Gita*, whose hero, Arjuna, suddenly loses the will to fight in a fratricidal war, and has to be persuaded to do so by his divine charioteer Krishna.

Gandhi was not alone in seeing this war as the greatest manifestation of a *dharma yuddha*, to which he returned frequently for inspiration.

Rather than representing the end or limit of moral action, the battlefield was for Gandhi its true home. Perhaps because moralists tend to describe warfare as the instantiation of all vice, thus depending upon the fear it inspires to justify their arguments, the Mahatma, who thought fearlessness the essence of virtue, chose to locate morality on the battlefield instead. In doing so he dismissed the political ideal of a state at peace as a good example of righteousness, even letting go of otherwise much invoked models like Rama the king as a personification of virtue, or his capital of Ayodhya as its privileged site. But then the ideal of *ramrajya*, or Rama's rule, with which Gandhi is so often associated, should not be seen as a political category in either its traditional or modern senses, since Rama here was not a king so much as a son, brother, father and husband. More importantly he was the hero of sacrifice, willing even to have his own wife suffer and die in the name of duty, and therefore a model for everyday life. Similarly war is not given over to politics in the Mahatma's telling of the *Gita*, and is often rendered into a spiritual struggle, as if in recognition of the fact that a state at war no longer represents even its own political ideals, though it might claim to be defending them. Lying at the heart of politics while at the same time constituting its outer limits, war has the paradoxical status of being political and anti-political at the same time, even threatening the dissolution of politics altogether, and in all these ways it serves as the most appropriate arena for moral action considered as a far more protean and universal form of human behavior. It is this form of action that Gandhi focused upon when thinking about the place of morality in the shadow of politics, which he did most powerfully in a commentary on the *Bhagavad-Gita* delivered at the Satyagraha Ashram in 1926.

THE IMPOSSIBLE INDIAN

The death of non-violence

I will return to Gandhi's commentary on Arjuna's dilemma in another section of this chapter, and begin instead with a remark made towards the end of his lengthy interpretation of the *Bhagavad-Gita*, which was made piecemeal during its public reading over several days at the ashram:

> Following the death of non-violence, we discovered the value of the spinning-wheel, as also of *brahmacharya* [celibacy]. Beyond the river (Sabarmati) is *bhogabhumi* [the site of passivity], while this is *karmabhumi* [the site of action].[5]

Notable about this comment are the two distinctions it makes: the first between nonviolence and spinning or celibacy, and the second between these practices of the ashram and those of the life beyond. How is nonviolence different from spinning or celibacy? Why do these practices make of the ashram a site of action compared with the world outside as one of passivity? Nonviolence, says Gandhi, was something negative and had no existence of its own. Unlike violence, which sought to have an effect as instrumental action, nonviolence did not plan, produce or achieve anything, but rather made change possible by withdrawing from such action. Nonviolence, however, did not flee the world of cause and effect, but made possible the most spectacular changes in it, and this by a process of negation instead of affirmation. Nonviolence allowed for changes in the world of cause and effect by setting up ever newer arenas of withdrawal in a manner deliberately opposed to the instrumental action so beloved of politics. Nonviolence, indeed, was so little a positive entity, let alone a political strategy, that Gandhi saw it as a kind of epistemological quality, one whose detachment he defined as an effect of truth:

> Truth is a positive value, while non-violence is a negative value. Truth affirms. Non-violence forbids something which is real enough. Truth exists, untruth does not exist. Violence exists, non-violence does not. Even

so, the highest dharma [duty] for us is that nothing but non-violence can be. Truth is its own proof, and non-violence is its supreme fruit. The latter is necessarily contained in the former.[6]

Now the comparisons made in the passage above, between truth and violence as positive objects and untruth and nonviolence as negative ones, suggest that Gandhi had come to see a series of complicated entanglements among them which no longer permitted of easy distinctions. This becomes clear in an example of violence that Gandhi gives from the *Gita*, that of Karna, Bhishma and Drona, all good men who yet sided with the evil prince Duryodhana in his battle against his cousins the Pandavas:

Whether out of compassion for Duryodhana, or because he was generous-hearted, Karna joined the former's side. Besides Karna, Duryodhana had good men like Bhishma and Drona also on his side. This suggests that *evil cannot by itself flourish in this world*. It can do so only if it is allied with some good. This was the principle underlying non-co-operation, that the evil system which the Government represents, and which has endured only because of the support it receives from good people, cannot survive if that support is withdrawn. Just as the Government needs the support of good men in order to exist, so Duryodhana required men like Bhishma and Drona in order to show that there was justice on his side.[7]

Gandhi's use of this example to illustrate non-cooperation as a form of nonviolence is curious, since the good men supporting Duryodhana did not after all withdraw their support of him, so that the evil of the Kauravas could only be defeated in a war of extreme violence, which the Mahatma elsewhere calls a righteous one.[8] The problem was not simply that good men refused to withdraw from evil, but that evil itself, or rather the violence it gave rise to, was also a product of goodness and inextricable from it. Here, in the mutual entanglement of truth and violence, untruth and nonviolence, might be found the latter's cause of death. This was why it became imperative to think about action and its inevitable violence in greater detail, because nonviolence alone was capable neither of replacing nor even of comprehending it. In other words the task Gandhi set himself in his interpretation of the *Bhagavad-Gita* was not to avoid action, or even its inevitable violence, but to attend upon its very materiality in a sort of phenomenology.

Spinning and celibacy, we saw earlier, provided the Mahatma with illustrations of moral action, having been chosen as experiments for his inquiries into its nature. Experiment, of course, was the English word Gandhi used to describe the various practices, such as non-cooperation or nonviolence, which he promoted from time to time as ways of being faithful to the truth. Like the practice of nonviolence, spinning and celibacy were also not instrumental activities, being meant neither to produce homespun cloth in the first instance, nor to endow the body with some unusual power in the second. Indeed Gandhi speaks of these practices without once mentioning anything they are supposed to produce, since it is precisely their character as disengaged actions that he is interested in. This is especially true of celibacy, which most clearly exits the instrumental logic of purpose and production, cause and effect, that for Gandhi marks the nature of violence, and of politics in particular as a practice of violence:

> If destruction is violence, creation, too, is violence. Procreation, therefore, involves violence. The creation of what is bound to perish certainly involves violence.[9]

Unlike practices of nonviolence, however, spinning and celibacy are not negatively conceived, but important in their own right as experiments in freedom. What is more they are the most material and weighty of actions, because disengaged from the idealizing imperative of instrumental thought, for which every act has meaning only in terms of some vision of the future, whether as cause or effect, purpose or product. Indeed violence might well represent the real outcome of such unreal acts that take leave of their own materiality to try and control the future. So in his example from the *Gita* invoked earlier, it becomes clear that for Gandhi Duryodhana's plan to annihilate the Pandavas is violent because it is unreal, relying as it does on the support of good men like Karna, Bhishma or Drona, whose purposes in supporting the Kauravas were very different from his own. In fact the Mahatma suggests that these men fought under Duryodhana's banner for completely non-political reasons, including compassion and generosity, which gave their actions materiality and so goodness. The point here being that actions intending to control the future are not only perfectly ideal in themselves, but ideal also because they can never quite control even their own instruments.

By this point a typically Gandhian reversal has been effected, and we realize that the very peculiarity of his concerns with spinning or celibacy in fact represents the peculiar materiality of everyday life, which forever escapes the idealizing violence of instrumental action, itself another name for politics. Spinning and celibacy are therefore practices in the materiality of action as a characteristic of everyday life, intended to restore to all action its gravity or existential weight. But this is by no means a nostalgic or even desperate effort to retain some old-fashioned materiality within the abstract politics of modernity. Indeed we might even say the opposite, that the increasing idealization of modern politics actually makes the materiality of action more disruptive and powerful. In any case the Mahatma is adamant about the intractable nature of such materiality, which he merely brings to political consciousness by offering it up as a sacrifice to the latter's idealism. In other words everyday action can only protect itself from politics by attending to its own materiality, just as politics can only protect itself from its own idealism by recognizing the intractable nature of action's everyday materiality.

But the act is material in more ways than lacking instrumentality, which as I have described it thus far may quite rightly be confused with a lack of motive or intention. What makes an action instrumental is neither motive nor intention, but the illusion that it might be absolutely created and absolutely controlled: that it might therefore be a sovereign act in the peculiarly theological sense this word has for modern politics. As the fantasy of a creation from out of the void, such action may characterize monotheistic thought, but is opposed by the notion of *karma*, action seen to be completely determined by a chain of cause and effect which begins before the actor's birth and continues well after his death. I shall return to this notion of action as part of a pre-determined universe illustrated by the idea of rebirth, as well as to the role it plays in Gandhi's interpretation of the *Bhagavad-Gita*. For the moment it suffices to note the following irony: that the act can only accede to its materiality and thus also its autonomy if it is limited, contingent and determined by the weight of a past rather than the idealism of a future. In other words action enjoys its materiality and autonomy only if it is separated from the instrumental thought that would idealize it, and it retains its separateness only insofar as it finds itself in a universe of determinations and is so unfree. Gandhi's phenomenology of the act is about precisely this unfreedom of everyday action, which he reflects upon in the concept of authority as the one form of determination that is moral rather than merely brutish in its force.

The paradox of authority

Now the paradox of authority is that it commands and forbids choice at the same moment, in effect demanding that a moral actor dignify his will by exercising it once only in the decision to obey. The weightiness of this choice, says the Mahatma, lends it a reality unknown to those who choose lightly and out of self-indulgence:

The action of a man whose intellect is not fixed on one aim, who is not single-minded in his devotion, will branch out in many directions. As the mind leaps, monkey-fashion, from branch to branch, so does the intellect. A person who clings to his life will seek help from any *vaid* or saint or witch-doctor whom he meets. Similarly, a monkey will fly from branch to branch and ultimately meet an untimely death, the victim of a sling-shot. The mind of a person of uncertain purpose grows weak day by day and becomes so unsettled that he can think of nothing except what is in his mind at the moment.[10]

Choice, therefore, becomes unreal by repetition and ends up as a purely mental fixation on self-gratification. Giving it up to authority, however, allows choice access to reality by freeing its agent from good as well as evil, seen as objects to which the moral actor is attached, and in whose name he justifies his action:

We say that we should offer up everything to God, even evil. The two, good and evil, are inseparable, and so we should offer up both. If we wish to give up sin, we should give up virtue too. There is possessiveness in clinging even to virtue.[11]

Authority, then, in giving the act its materiality and autonomy in the most everyday manner, by the same token gives it a kind of freedom as well. And it is the authoritative nature of this freedom that the Mahatma proceeds to study in his interpretation of the *Bhagavad-Gita*.

It should now be evident why Gandhi, in the statement I first quoted from him, distinguished nonviolence from spinning or celibacy on the one hand, and on the other described these practices of the ashram as active ones, compared to the passive practices of the world beyond. His commentary on the *Gita* conducts a phenomenological examination of the act's materiality, in terms of what he considered to be its necessary relationship with an authority that alone bestows upon it some measure of freedom. And while such speculations might seem at times arcane, it is worth repeating that they insistently take everyday life as their subject, and deal with it in the most quotidian of ways. Indeed it was the Mahatma's frequent self-description as a crank, and his very obsession with what he often called fads, such as fasting, spinning or celibacy, that put his concerns squarely at the center of everyday life. And this is not even to mention his immense popularity, which to this day brooks no rival anywhere in the Subcontinent. But why think about action, authority and freedom through a reading of the *Bhagavad-Gita*? The suitability of its content apart, it was the sacred authority of the text that drew Gandhi to it: not because the *Gita* was in fact such an authority, but because its reading allowed Gandhi to pose authority itself as a question for all action. It goes without saying that posed as it was in a reading of the *Gita*, this question enabled the Mahatma to address the nature of action in his typically indirect way, as if from outside the arena of politics.

Of course the *Gita* had been an important text for modern Hinduism since the nineteenth century, especially among nationalists and religious reformers. (The names Vivekananda, Tilak and Aurobindo immediately come to mind.)[12] With these men, keenly interested in their country's political life, the text seems to have functioned as an authority alternative to that of politics seen in the traditional terms of *artha* or power. Is it possible that given their political subjection during this period, the *Bhagavad-Gita* allowed these men to distinguish authority from power in a way that refused even to define the former as a legitimate form of the latter? Whatever the case, such colonial interpretations of the *Gita* brought to the fore a thinking of ethics rather than of politics. But the fact that it is war that provides the arena of moral action, rather than simply its limits, for the *Bhagavad-Gita* as much as for its colonial interpreters, suggests that this ethics was not meant to be something inner or spiritual as juxtaposed with the outer or material world of the state. Indeed we shall see with Gandhi that morality addressed the politics of the state precisely by undoing these divisions of inner and outer, spiritual and material, which were all products of the latter's modernity.

For Gandhi, then, the *Bhagavad-Gita* was neither history nor scripture, and certainly not philosophy. To begin with, the

Mahatma always made it clear that far from being a symbol of pre-colonial authenticity, the text for him was completely mediated by his first reading of its English translation while a student in London:

> It was at this time that, coming into contact with two Englishmen, I was induced to read the *Gita*: I say "induced" because I had no particular desire to read it. When these two friends asked me to read the *Gita* with them, I felt rather ashamed. The consciousness that I knew nothing about our holy books made me feel miserable. The reason, I think, was my vanity. I did not know Sanskrit well enough to be able to read the *Gita* without help. The two English friends, on their part, did not know Sanskrit at all. They gave me Sir Edwin Arnold's excellent translation of the poem. I went through the whole of it immediately and was fascinated by it.[13]

In any case, continues Gandhi, the book is not a work of history, and this for both epistemological and ethical reasons:

> The Mahabharata is not a history; it is a dharma-grantha [holy book]. Who can ever describe an actual event? A man cannot exactly describe even a drop of water seen by him. God having created him so weak, how can he describe an actual event perfectly. In this battle, moreover, the warriors were, on the one side, the sons of Dharma, Vayu, Indra and Ashvini-kumars and, on the other, a hundred brothers all born at the same instant. Have we ever heard of such a thing actually happening? Duryodhana rode on the chariot of adharma, and Arjuna that of dharma. The battle described here is, therefore, a struggle between dharma and adharma.[14]

As far as its status as scripture is concerned, Gandhi claims that the *Gita* is not a particularly Hindu book but rather a non-sectarian teaching of ethics:

> This is a work which persons belonging to all faiths can read. It does not favor any sectarian point of view. It teaches nothing but pure ethics.[15]

Far from being a book of revelation in the monotheistic sense, it is actually a second-order source of authority, important only because one cannot find true gurus or preceptors in the present age. The text is important, in other words, not as a source of revelation, since it is not in fact capable of solving the problems of everyday life, but instead as an authority for everyday action:

If by Shastra we mean a book, the Bible, the Koran and other books have been before mankind for so many hundreds of years, but no-one has come to the end of these problems. The intention of this verse is to tell us not to look upon ourselves as an authority, that is, not to be guided by our wishes and feelings.[16]

What does it mean for the *Bhagavad-Gita* to be an authority? For one thing, it means that the text is not a work of philosophy but one whose very externality allows individuals to judge their actions in its terms, and in doing so to form a community of interpreters whose debates over the text submit the actions of each one of them to examination. For the Mahatma, therefore, the *Gita*, like the unavailable guru, is an authority chosen and even interpreted, though not in a way that sets specialized learning over the generality of moral action that is available to all:

Simple like a villager that I am, why should I insist on reading the *Gita* myself? Why should Mahadev refuse to do that? Why did I take this upon myself? Because I have the necessary humility. I believe that we are all imperfect in one way or another. But I know well enough what dharma means, and have tried to follow it in my life. If I have somewhere deep in me the spirit of dharma and loving devotion to God, I shall be able to kindle it in you.[17]

As an external authority the *Bhagavad-Gita* creates a community of interpreters by preventing subjects from speaking in their own names. It also prevents the actions of these subjects from being idealized in the instrumentality of political life, thus giving them both freedom and materiality. This is why Gandhi was so insistent upon maintaining the externality of the *Gita*, prescribing for its recitation all manner of ritual attentions, because it was "necessary to create an atmosphere of holiness round the *Gita*".[18] Yet at the end of the day he had to confess that the book alone offered no help:

The conclusion of our study of the *Gita* is that we should pray and read holy books, and know our duty and do it. If any book can help, it is this. Really, however, what help can a book or a commentary on it give?[19]

The point of authority, therefore, was neither its power nor its truth but merely its externality. This comes through very clearly in that part of Gandhi's commentary on the *Gita* where he suddenly describes a Protestant named Wallace, who experimented with Hinduism before turning Roman Catholic and accepting the authority of the Pope:

If the Pope is immoral, there is bound to be corruption in society, but any person who has decided that he will do nothing on his own but do only what the Pope asks him to do, will only benefit himself. A Protestant would say that one should obey one's conscience, but this Wallace kept his conscience out and surrendered himself to the Pope. His giving up concern for his conscience was a great idea.[20]

Given his frequent and favorable invocations of conscience elsewhere, the Mahatma's rejection of this virtue here might be read not as a denial of what he called the "inner voice", but his criticism of any notion of conscience that abandons externality altogether to become self-possessed and so self-indulgent.[21] This is why Gandhi was not interested in a book called the *Bhagavad-Gita* or even in its message, but rather in the kind of moral action that the external authority they represented made possible, such externality being a prerequisite for the autonomy and materiality of action. His reading of the *Gita* was therefore nothing more than an exploration in the nature of action.

Virtue out of necessity

The setting for Gandhi's exploration of moral action was Arjuna's celebrated dilemma on the battlefield of Kurukshetra. Arjuna's dilemma, according to the Mahatma, was not whether he should or should not kill his relatives, but how any choice he might make in the circumstances would be at all meaningful morally. After all, whether he killed or did not, a slaughter would in any case ensue, and one in which he was fully implicated. How, then, could Arjuna either claim or avoid responsibility by any choice he might make? Or as Gandhi puts it:

> Let us suppose that Arjuna flees the battlefield. Though his enemies are wicked people, are sinners, they are his relations and he cannot bring himself to kill them. If he leaves the field, what would happen to those vast numbers on his side? If Arjuna went away, leaving them behind, would the Kauravas have mercy on them? If he left the battle, the Pandava army would be simply annihilated. What, then, would be the plight of their wives and children? [...] If Arjuna had left the battlefield, the very calamities which he feared would have befallen them. Their families would have been ruined, and the traditional dharma of these families and the race would have been destroyed. Arjuna, therefore, had no choice but to fight.[22]

The question here is therefore the opposite of that normally asked in discussions of ethics: not how one should exercise choice, but how an act might retain moral meaning in a situation where choice itself has become superfluous. And choice becomes superfluous only in a world where every act includes what it intends as well as its opposite, thus giving rise to violence. Such a totality could be addressed neither by a calculus of means and ends nor by the arbitrariness of conscience, but instead, Gandhi thought, by action that abandoned choice altogether, which was after all meaningless if it could not determine the future. For only action that gave up the myth of control or effect might occur within a universe of determinations without itself falling prey to the sublime character of its totality.

Starting with the criticism that moral choice was delusionary and self-indulgent, Gandhi went on to reject its unacknowledged politics, by which such choice was held to determine the future and so retrospectively justify itself, just as ends are said to justify means. But how was choice or will to be eliminated from moral behavior? For one thing by rejecting the quest for self-realization upon which it was so often predicated in an ostentatious disavowal of crass instrumentality. Though a votary of self-realization at other times, the Mahatma was deeply suspicious of its narcissistic potential in his commentary on the *Gita*, because he thought that such a concern deprived action of its gravity by turning it into one among many options in an endless quest for fulfillment. Self-realization as a spiritual activity should therefore be replaced by self-purification as a bodily one:

> We discussed yesterday that we should speak not of "self-realization" but of "self-purification". Self-purification is to be achieved through the body. We act through the *atman* [soul] to the degree that we act through the body. In truth, however, the *atman* does nothing, nor does it cause anything to be done.[23]

In other words self-realization was only possible by way of bodily action as a form of self-purification, since the self did not exist without a body that determined it:

> All this talk about knowledge is because of the body; otherwise, for an unembodied one, how can there be any question of knowledge? The highest knowledge of all in the world is knowledge of the self. Moreover, the idea of a human being having no body exists only in our imagination. Mortification of the body, therefore, is the only means of self-realization and the only *yajna* [sacrifice] for everyone in the world.[24]

Running against the current of moral thought down the ages, this was an extraordinary attack on the supposedly free subject of ethics, conceived in terms of a spiritual or mental self that remained unhampered by the body. It was also an attack on the knowledge that gave substance to the freedom of such an ethical subject. Both attacks were prompted at least in part by Gandhi's recognition that this self and its knowledge were necessarily confined to a few adepts alone, serving at most only as ideals for the rest and not therefore the stuff of everyday morality. But it is important to note that the Mahatma did not reject this form of ethics because it was difficult for the generality of people;

indeed he thought them capable of far more in the way of sacrifice than anything prescribed a moral elite by the votaries of self-realization. What he objected to was the fact that such aristocratic forms of ethical life depended upon luxuries like time and learning that were not available to most. But more than this he thought that selfhood could not exist apart from the body and that knowledge was never adequate to the choice required of it. And so Gandhi had to eliminate moral choice altogether by sacrificing its agent and knowledge to action as a process of forgetting. This involved disciplining oneself to behave in such a way as to make morality something habitual and spontaneous, in the same way as the body functioned automatically and was so free:

> When a man's ears, nose, eyes, and so on, go on performing their functions naturally without conscious willing on his part—the winking of the eyelids does not need to be willed, there must be some disease if it is otherwise—we say of such a person that his sense organs, having become free of attachments and aversions, function spontaneously.[25]

Having in this marvelous way turned willing into a disease and revealed the body as a site of freedom at least in this instance, the Mahatma went on to recommend that the latter's spontaneity be extended to moral life by a practice of forgetting that was both familiar and easily available:

> When typing on a typewriter has become mechanical work with the typist, the finger will alight on the right letter even when he is not looking at the keyboard; he who is able to work in such a spontaneous manner and is fully alert, like the typist, in everything he does, may be described as the Buddha.[26]

But forgetting has to do with more than spontaneous action, and involves putting even the objects of one's morality out of mind, so that these latter cannot become part of some bargain in which one good deed is repaid by another. For this orientation of an act to the future would simply smuggle politics back into ethics by an obscure back door:

BROTHERS IN ARMS

We should not serve anyone with the hope that he, too, will serve us one day, but we may serve him because the Lord dwells in him and we serve that Lord. If we hear anyone crying in distress for help, we should immediately run to him and help him. We should help the Lord crying in distress. After doing what was needed, we should feel that it was all a dream. Would the Lord ever cry in distress?[27]

Though it seems far-fetched, Gandhi's advice in the passage above offers us a way of dissociating moral action from the politics of reciprocal obligation and contract, which entails forgetting ethical relations and therefore rejecting any community based upon them. This was certainly the Mahatma's way of avoiding all action motivated by sentimental reasons like pity, horror and even hatred, each deriving from an imagination exercised by stories of needless suffering. So while he advocated the display of suffering voluntarily undergone, Gandhi thought that it could only inspire admiration in the hearts of observers, and prompt their conversion to the sufferer's cause, rather than calling forth passions stoked up by tales of victimization and the obligations of charity as much as revenge they implied. Indeed as responses to suffering, charity and revenge used the same language and thus amounted to the same thing, which was perhaps why one could so easily turn into the other. Quite unsentimental himself, Gandhi remained levelheaded during the most tumultuous of times, refusing to enter into what he thought of as a political relationship of pity and gratitude with his interlocutors.

Action without a subject

All this meant that the traditional figure of the moral subject, constituted by will and freed from bodily dependency, had to be replaced by someone quite different. Gandhi chose as his moral exemplars the figures of the child and the slave, who had in the past, a few religious ideals apart, served as the very emblems of moral lack. While criticizing the unhealthy effect that slavery had upon the master, who was after all tied to his slave by self-interest, the Mahatma saw in the latter someone who could forget himself because he was unable to exercise choice:

> The slave can never conceive of his existence without his master. A person who has the name of another on his lips all the twenty-four hours will forget himself in the latter. The *atman* [individual soul] becomes the *paramatman* [universal soul] in the same manner.[28]

The slave, then, becomes for Gandhi the model of a moral subject, as indeed he was for a number of religious traditions in India and beyond. Similarly children were examples of virtue because they alone could be counted as truly free, their physical, and even intellectual or spiritual needs all being taken care of by adults, so that they could live non-politically in the immediate present:

> If children have faith, they can live as a *sthitaprajna* [one who is single-minded or self-possessed] does. They have their parents and teachers to look after their needs. They have, therefore, no need to take thought for themselves. They should always be guided by their elders. A child who lives in this manner is a *brahmachari* [celibate or unattached person], a *muni* [saint], a *sthitaprajna*. He is so in the sense that he does what he is asked to and carries out every instruction.[29]

By locating traditional virtues like freedom and faith, to say nothing of celibacy and asceticism, in the unexpected figures of children and slaves, Gandhi was doing more than pointing out the superficiality and contradictions of older ethical models. He was also attempting to universalize moral ideals in non-hierarchical ways and see them at work in every aspect of social life. This did not of course mean that the Mahatma glorified slavery and advised obedience to all authority. Indeed his own life was dedicated precisely to contesting such authority, whether in the form of politics or religion, and, however imperfectly, he might be seen to have done so. Obedience was important because it was a necessary and inevitable part of social life in general. And if anything it was more important for moral life in particular, since even an ethics founded upon conscience requires obedience to the call of one's better self if it is to function. Instead of seeing in obedience merely a limit to moral action, in other words, Gandhi recognized it as an irreducible element of ethics, one whose virtue needed to be fostered in its own right, much as religions of various kinds had always done, though perhaps not for the same reasons. And in doing so he showed up the poverty of ethical principles as they are commonly understood, confined as they are to a moral aristocracy while prevaricating about crucial features of social life, obedience being only the most obvious instance of these.

While children and slaves might have provided models of virtue for the Mahatma, he did not think that moral subjects were all the same, and possessed no generic idea about them. On the contrary he defined their obligations in the most multifarious ways by citing the old notion of *swadharma* (individual duty), according to which people belonging to different castes, genders and generations each had their own particular role to play, also therefore owing obedience to particular authorities.[30] Opposed to the standardized subject of modern law, and therefore of politics as well, *swadharma* could not be determined by others but only decided for oneself.[31] And its task was not simply to differentiate one's own duty from that of others, but also to distinguish among the recipients of one's action. This ostensibly unequal treatment, both of oneself and of others, produces real equality in an almost communist sense, as in the famous shibboleth "from each according to his ability, to each according to his needs". And it does so by turning the subject who distinguishes and differentiates into someone who by that very token is *samadarshi*, able to see everything equally:

When can we say of a person that he is *samadarshi*? Can we say so of that man who would give equal quantities to an elephant and an ant? Indeed no. We can say it of him who gives to each according to his or her need.[32]

The test of equal regard, however, as of moral action in general, was undoubtedly sacrifice, which Gandhi prized above knowledge, freedom and the like because it was the only moral form available to everyone without distinction. Indeed the bulk of his commentary on the *Gita* is taken up with a discussion of sacrifice, whether it is called spinning, celibacy, fasting or dying. For the *Bhagavad-Gita*, of course, it is not dying but killing that is seen as the ultimate sacrifice, in its own way much more arduous than dying when it involves killing one's relatives. Though in principle opposed to killing, the Mahatma did see it as being unavoidable on certain occasions, for instance when it came to protecting the weak, though even here he preferred dying as a protective act.[33] But his approbation of killing went much further when describing Arjuna's dilemma:

> The *Gita* permits no distinction between one's relatives and others. If one must kill, one should kill one's people first. Shri Krishna asks Arjuna: "What is this you are saying about people being your relations?" The *Gita* wants to free him from this ignorant distinction of some people being his relations and others not. He has resolved to kill. It was not right, then, that he should shrink from killing particular individuals.[34]

The duty enunciated by *swadharma* required that one's own relatives be killed before anybody else, this proof of detachment and equal regard being the truest way in which killing could partake of morality. Such forms of killing even represented the most sublime of moral acts, because they entailed greater sacrifices than merely dying for others. And so Gandhi repeatedly praised the sacrificial killings, whether only intended or actually carried out, that were ascribed to heroic or saintly figures like Arjuna, Harischandra and Prahlad, though he did not of course recommend the practice among his contemporaries. How did the apostle of nonviolence come to see killing as the highest form of sacrifice, and therefore as the supreme moral act? The process of reasoning that led him to this conclusion was driven by a desire for universality: ethics was either possible everywhere and available to everyone or it had no meaning at all. We have already seen how this desire informed the Mahatma's rejection of choice, knowledge and self-realization for authority, obedience and self-purification. It is because he did not think any morality worthwhile that abdicated responsibility in situations of extreme violence, or had to be confined to a moral aristocracy, that Gandhi ended up investing traditional moral categories like authority and sacrifice with a universality they had not previously possessed. For his idea of ethical universality was fundamentally egalitarian in nature, and thus tied to the politics of anti-colonialism, though without partaking of its instrumentality, which bartered the virtues of the present for ideals of freedom and equality in the future.

This is the sense in which Gandhi's morality can be said to exist in the shadow of politics, whose practices it had perforce to engage if with the gravest of doubts. Rather than simply an inheritance from some Indian past, therefore, his deployment of traditional moral categories, all transformed in the process, might be recognized as an effort to avoid those, like legal freedom and equality, that provide the currency of modern politics. And this was important not because politics was altogether evil, but because it was founded upon an instrumentality that sacrificed the present for the future, thus denying the former its existential weight while robbing all action of reality. The Mahatma's alternative, then, was to sacrifice the future for the present, in the firm belief that the former would better be secured by attending to the latter's virtue. Controlling the present, after all, was more feasible than predicting the future, which was one reason why self-purification and sacrifice were so crucial for Gandhi, and part of the same logic as his otherwise inexplicable rejection of locomotives and fast cars, which he thought deprived their passengers precisely of a lived present.

Indeed the Mahatma can be said to have inhabited the present more fully than any thinker or man of action in the last century, and to have invested it with more significance than it had ever possessed, if only by replacing the fleeting and illusory character of this category with a gravity appropriate to modern times. And so to become arenas for moral action, war and killing had also to be diverted from their orientation to the future and made fully present. For Gandhi saw in the battlefield not an exception to ethics but the very stuff of its reality, if only because it provided a site for moral action that politics could not occupy without risking self-destruction. Instead of withdrawing from such violence, then, moral action had to prove its mettle by domesticating and even going beyond it, to occupy an arena such as Arjuna did on the battlefield of Kurukshetra, where politics might not venture because choice had been rendered superfluous there. Only by exceeding its future-making violence in this way would politics finally be cast in morality's shadow:

> In this world which baffles our reason, violence there will then always be. The *Gita* shows us the way which will lead us out of it, but it also says that we cannot escape it simply by running away from it like cowards. Anyone who prepares to run away would do better, instead, to kill and be killed.[35]

It is a rare thing in the history of moral thought when even its most sublime of notions come to possess quotidian realities, but Gandhi may be said to have enjoyed the good fortune, if such it can be called, of seeing his gravest of thoughts come to life before his own eyes. I want to close this chapter on the Mahatma's moral thought, then, with an example of such a reality, specifically one that has to do with the virtue of fratricide so important in his reading of the *Gita*. While Gandhi often cited scriptural examples of such terrifying virtues, and sometimes even referred to his own forms of non-cooperation with close relatives as slighter instances of them, every so often the stuff of Indian politics presented him with the genuine article like a gift. And in these gifts the last few months of his life were particularly rich, spent as they were working for nonviolence in the murderous context of India's partition. The Mahatma's last fasts and their startling effect in reducing this violence, to say nothing about his death, which stopped its expansion altogether, are well known, but I want to focus here on a single promise of fratricide as the most exceptional of virtues.

The anthropologist Nirmal Kumar Bose, who had served as Gandhi's secretary during the time he spent in Bengal in 1946 and 1947, recounts the following story from the latter year, when attacks were being launched against Muslims who remained in Calcutta following the carving out of East Pakistan from its hinterland. The so-called "Miracle of Calcutta", when the Mahatma appeared to have stopped the mutual killing of Hindus and Muslims at the risk of his own life, appeared to have become a thing of the past. And the fleeing members of each community, whom he had persuaded to return to the localities in which they had been minorities, while charging their more numerous neighbors to protect them, were again beginning to fear for their safety. Just as Gandhi was discussing the possibility of organizing this evacuation, a truck with some thirty departing Muslims passed by his camp and was attacked by two hand grenades thrown at it. Sometime later Bose met a number of the young Hindu militants from whose group the attackers had come. Showing him around the neighborhood with the few elderly Muslims who remained in it unharmed, they had the following discussion with the Mahatma's secretary:

The young men said that although a small batch from among them had erred and hurled the fatal bomb on the refugee truck, yet they themselves would request Gandhiji to stop any further evacuation. It was a point of honor with them, after they had given their word a few days ago to Gandhiji, to protect the remaining Mussulmans from further harm. And for this purpose they might even have to use sten guns at night; only they would request Gandhiji to advise the Police not to arrest anybody in possession of unlicensed arms. I listened to them and then reported the whole matter to Gandhiji. Gandhiji gave a most unexpected reply. He asked me to tell the young men that 'he was with them. If Prafulla Babu, the Chief

Minister, could not protect the minority with his government forces, and the young men decided to do so, they deserved his support'.[36]

It is of course possible to interpret the young men's actions as an attempt to keep their weapons and have numbers of Muslims at hand from whom they might extort valuables or indeed merely for the sake of humiliating them. But in taking these young men at their word, Gandhi was doing more than asking them to take the place of a government unable to protect its citizens. For the logic of the discussion between Bose and the militants was not in the least political, dealing only with the fulfillment of a promise made to the Mahatma, and certainly not with any legalistic recognition of the "right" of Muslims to live unmolested by their neighbors. Even more important, we can imagine, was the fact that these young men were willing to kill their own brothers in order to fulfill their obligations, which is probably why Gandhi never thought of asking them to resist nonviolently. Here, then, was surely demonstration of a truth the Mahatma had learnt from the *Bhagavad-Gita*, that morality survives where politics cannot, its universality tested and found true in the willingness to kill rather than simply to die. For when it is embodied in the willingness to slay one's brothers, morality is able to snatch even killing from the grasp of a politics that requires this act for its very definition. And it is in this way that fratricide represents the triumph of morality over politics.

5

HITLER'S CONVERSION

There is something curious about the enduring popularity of a fascist classic like *Mein Kampf* in India, with second-hand copies of the text being sold to a mass audience on the pavements of megacities like Mumbai, and this despite its denigrating references to Indians. The book's author enjoys a similar popularity among Indians who are not necessarily fascists or even conversant with the movement's European past. In fact it is precisely because Hitler has become history, and is no longer connected to any major political party or movement that he can serve for these fans as a representative of worldwide might in the most generic fashion. And yet even during its heyday in the 1930s and 40s fascism was appropriated for rather different ends in countries like India, which as European colonies had themselves to deal with racial exclusion and alien rule, both set in place by those who claimed during the Second World War to be fighting Nazism in the name of freedom and equality. Notwithstanding the significant differences between fascism and imperialism, in other words, it was difficult in such places to draw a clear historical line separating one from the other. And so fascism could be accepted or rejected in India by the same token as the ideology of a colonial power, or later a Cold War superpower might.

Whatever the source of its popularity in India, this unwillingness to think about fascism in Manichaean terms tells us that Nazism in particular was very likely appropriated there as part of the general history of Europe, one that included colonialism and much else besides, rather than because it represented a radical negation of all that was civilized about that continent. Fascism's Indian legacy, then, would among other things serve as an illustration of her people's tolerance of diverse political trends, as well as their openness to the outside world, instead of being seen as promoting only the violent task of creating a purified nation. Indeed it is possible to say that even those Indians who are truly fascist in their methods and aims have to struggle against Nazism's popular appropriation in order to preserve its radical character. For fascist themes in India have come to characterize religious movements, both Hindu and Muslim, as well as secular ones, to constitute a political language of the most general kind. My purpose in this chapter, then, is to sketch the history of India's engagement with fascism and show how its character allowed Gandhi to mount an entirely novel criticism of Nazi politics during the Second World War.

Fascism with Indian characteristics

Nazism shares a peculiar history with India, one whose beginnings might be traced to the eighteenth century, when Sir William Jones's discovery that north Indian languages were part of the same family as western European ones was turned into a racial theory of common Aryan origins. In the nineteenth century this theory was elaborated by linguists and anthropologists and came to focus on the problem of racial purity. The Brahmins, therefore, who in their priestly exclusiveness might once have been compared to Jews, were now seen as the descendants of pre-historical Aryan invaders who had subjugated the Subcontinent's lesser peoples, attempting to ensure

HITLER'S CONVERSION

their dominance by sanctifying the proscriptions of caste.[1] These speculations had enormous influence in India, with Hindu reformers downplaying racial divisions among the country's caste and regional groups, while at the same time stressing the ancient unity of Indians and Europeans, which made Muslims rather than Jews into Semitic interlopers in the homeland of the Aryans. The Nazis, of course, inherited many of these Indian themes, including a fascination with the Himalayas as an Aryan redoubt and with Sanskrit texts like the *Bhagavad-Gita* as examples of racial ethics.

But India also played another and quite converse role in the fascist imagination, as a testament to the virtues of British imperialism. For Hitler saw India as the greatest example of Aryan dominance in modern times, and sought to reproduce British colonial practices in Europe conceived of as a fascist empire.[2] This double history bound India and Nazi Germany together in such a way as to allow Hindus to "recognize" fascism as a native growth, while at the same time permitting Muslims to see in it, as in British colonialism, a latter-day example of their own world-encompassing imperial mission.[3] Such convoluted histories made for a curious set of identifications, psychological as much as political, between Indians under colonial rule on the one hand and European ideologies on the other. So when the president of the Muslim League compared his co-religionists to the Sudeten Germans, a minority serving as the beachhead of much larger numbers abroad, his political enemy, the president of the Hindu Mahasabha, pointed out that a more apt comparison would be the German Jews, with whose fate he threatened India's Muslims.[4] After the war, and with the coming into being of Israel, Hindu nationalists changed their tune and began supporting the Jewish state against its Muslim enemies, though they have never quite abandoned their admiration of Hitler. And this only goes to show how variously fascism could be adopted and appropriated in India.

Although many of these historical identifications continue to be invoked in contemporary India, more important has been the view of fascism as being, like communism, a form of modernity alternative to liberalism and capitalism, both seen as being compromised by their relations with imperialism. The fact that both ideologies were anti-British lent them even more luster in the eyes of many Indians during the first half of the twentieth century, when fascism and communism looked like they represented the world's political future. While they might be political rivals, therefore, communism and fascism played a similar role in the imagination of many an Indian freedom fighter. Chief among these was Subhas Chandra Bose, the only one to lead a military assault against Britain, making use in this endeavor of his countrymen who had been taken prisoner by the Germans in North Africa or "liberated" by the Japanese in South-East Asia, though he was not averse to gaining Soviet assistance as well. Still a great national hero in India, whose brief meeting with Hitler is glorified as a sign of his international prestige, it would be wrong to describe Bose's movement as fascist despite his admiration of the Nazis, for in this case as in so many others the diffuse popularity of fascism in India ended up preventing its organized emergence there.[5] So there is nothing contradictory in the fact that a mural of Bose meeting Hitler adorns a wall of the Calcutta metro, commissioned though it was by the communist government of Bengal. After all Bose was only following in the footsteps of those who had in the past turned to other among Britain's enemies for help. These allies had included the French during the Napoleonic Wars and the Germans during the First World War. And then there were the Japanese, who had vanquished Russia in 1905 and were lauded as the first Asian power to defeat a European empire.

Despite the anti-colonial context within which fascism was placed in India, one that I have suggested militated against its radicalism, the movement was taken up there on its own terms

HITLER'S CONVERSION

too. Apart from the small, mostly religious groups that actively advocated it, fascism in the 1930s and 40s was condemned by all of India's major political parties, with the Indian National Congress and Muslim League at the forefront, the first struggling for a united India and the latter for the autonomy and eventually the independence of its large Muslim minority. One of the ways they did this was by linking fascism with imperialism and indeed European modernity itself, as in the following statement broadcast by All-India Radio on New Year's Day 1938, by the period's pre-eminent Muslim ideologist, the poet and philosopher Mohammad Iqbal. Fascism, for Iqbal, had to be seen as the logical outcome of any political order founded upon the dominance of property, which he thought was safeguarded by the modern state, whatever its ideological hue:

> The modern age prides itself on its progress in knowledge and its matchless scientific developments. [...]. But in spite of all these developments, the tyranny of imperialism struts abroad, covering its face under the masks of Democracy, Nationalism, Communism, Fascism and heaven knows what else besides. Under these masks, in every corner of the earth, the spirit of freedom and the dignity of man are being trampled underfoot in a way to which not even the darkest period of human history presents a parallel. [...]. The rulers whose duty it was to protect and cherish those ideals which go to form a higher humanity, to prevent man's oppression of man and to elevate the moral and intellectual level of mankind, have in their hunger for dominion and imperial possessions, shed the blood of millions and reduced millions to servitude simply in order to pander to the greed and avarice of their own particular groups. After subjugating and establishing their dominion over weaker peoples, they have robbed them of their religions, their morals, of their cultural traditions and their literatures.[6]

Jawaharlal Nehru, Iqbal's contemporary and a leading light of the Congress, might have balked at comparing fascism to democracy, nationalism and communism, but he, too, agreed in linking it to imperialism in a book written in 1944, bemoaning the fact that even democratic nations were willing to sacrifice human well-being for their own self-interest.⁷ More particularly he pointed out that it was the imperial policies of countries like Britain and France that prevented the conclusion of any general agreement on disarmament after the First World War, for instance by upholding the former's "right" to bomb civilian populations from the air in places like Iraq and India even when no war had been declared there, and in these ways setting in place the legal precedents and political conditions for Hitler's subsequent actions in Europe.⁸ Unlike Nehru, however, but in tune with many of his compatriots, Iqbal, though he condemned fascism wholeheartedly, was not immune to the fascination it exerted, and had earlier written a poem about Mussolini, described as the kind of dynamic leader who changed the course of his country's history, though he was unsure whether to call this transformation an awakening or merely a more profound form of sleep.⁹ These sentiments were sometimes reciprocated by the fascists themselves, as in 1931 when Mussolini met Gandhi in Rome while the latter was returning to India from the Round Table Conference in London, and used the occasion for propaganda purposes that deeply embarrassed the Congress.¹⁰

When they were not united in viewing fascism as belonging to the same political logic as imperialism, Indian leaders occupied themselves in accusing their rivals of being little more than Nazis. Thus Mohammad Ali Jinnah, president of the Muslim League and soon to be founder of Pakistan, bitterly castigated the Indian National Congress, which had come to power in much of British India following the 1937 elections, of being fascist in both principle and practice. Though he often alleged that Congress governments persecuted Muslim minorities in the provinces they ruled, Jinnah's accusations of the party's fascism were for the most part couched in constitutional terms. So he described Gandhi as a *fuehrer* who exercised an extraordinary influence upon the Congress, though he was not a member of that party and so unaccountable to it, his power deriving entirely from the kind of populism that enjoyed no constitutional warrant. Even the Congress High Command, claimed Jinnah, was nothing but a "grand fascist council", because it attempted to control the party's representatives in the provinces despite being itself an unelected body with no constitutional precedent. In a speech on 6 March 1940, delivered to the Muslim University Union at Aligarh, he had this to say:

> We cannot accept a system of government in which the non-Muslims merely by numerical majority would rule and dominate us. The question was put to me if I did not want democracy what then did I want—Fascism, Nazism or Totalitarianism? I say what have these votaries, these champions of democracy done? They have kept sixty millions of people as untouchables; they have set up a system which is nothing but a Grand Fascist Council. Their dictator is not even a four-anna member of the Congress. They set up dummy ministries which were not responsible to the legislature or the electorate but to a caucus of Mr. Gandhi's choosing.[11]

Such accusations were also leveled against the Congress by British observers, and intellectuals like Reginald Coupland, who monitored the consequences of electoral politics in colonial India, worried about the party's drift towards fascist forms.[12] These suspicions were lent more credence when the Congress agitated against India being taken into the war without her people's consent, finally resigning office in protests that both the British and Indians belonging to parties like the Muslim League viewed as ill considered at best, and political blackmail to gain some unfair advantage at worst. Making common cause with Jinnah, some British commentators, such as the journalist Patrick Lacey, drew the now familiar comparison of India's Muslims to Germany's Jews, seeing the subcontinent as an Asiatic version of Europe, comprising a set of diverse national and religious groups forcibly united under the subjection of Hindu fascism.[13] For their part Indian nationalists were not slow in condemning the bad faith in which these rather convenient accusations were made by a colonial government intent on preserving its rule. They also described the Muslim League as being itself a fascist body, one that fomented violence between Hindus and Muslims to gain the latter's support, a party whose absolute dictator was none other than the self-styled constitutionalist Mohammad Ali Jinnah. In the *Discovery of India*, for instance, Nehru, after describing the Muslim League's unsubstantiated propaganda regarding Congress "atrocities" goes on to compare his political rivals with fascists:

> I had made a close study of Nazi methods of propaganda since Hitler's rise to power and I was astonished to find something similar taking place in India. A year later, in 1938, when Czechoslovakia had to face the Sudetenland crisis, the Nazi methods employed there were studied and referred to with approval by Moslem League spokesmen. A comparison was drawn between the position of Sudetenland Germans and Indian Moslems. Violence and incitements in speeches and in some newspapers became marked. A Congress Moslem minister was stabbed and there was no condemnation of this from any Moslem League leader; in fact it was condoned. Other exhibitions of violence frequently took place.[14]

It was in this context, where India's intimacy with European politics was matched by her alienation from them, that Gandhi's engagement with fascism occurred. Interestingly the Mahatma never referred to Indian debates about fascism, though like many of his countrymen he saw the latter as being of a piece with Europe's modernity, as much a part of it as democracy and imperialism. Rather than responding to allegations that fascist practices might be found in the Congress or the League, to say nothing of smaller parties like the Hindu Mahasabha, Gandhi's analysis was chiefly concerned with the challenge that such practices might pose his doctrine of nonviolent resistance. And indeed the most forceful and abiding of criticisms that Gandhi's methods have yet had to face is that they are unable to deal with fascist or totalitarian forms of oppression. Hannah Arendt's famous essay on violence illustrates perhaps the classical form this criticism takes, one whose irony it is to advocate the cause

HITLER'S CONVERSION

of a violence she abhorred against the Mahatma's form of non-violence.[15] Whether Arendt underestimated the violence of colonialism by attributing such success as Gandhi achieved to British forbearance, as Hitler himself imagined, or whether the Raj could not risk employing fascist methods in India without courting a general uprising, the Mahatma himself viewed Nazism as a challenge that had to be addressed.

Morality in a time of mass murder

Like all the challenges he encountered during a lengthy career, Gandhi saw in fascism a test as much as an opportunity for nonviolence. Though he was not interested, therefore, in making Nazism out to be an exceptional phenomenon falling outside the ken of nonviolence, neither was the Mahatma concerned with minimizing the unprecedented nature of its violence. Indeed he was keen to acknowledge this violence in as fulsome a way as possible so as to test the "matchless weapon of non-violence" against it. At the very commencement of war, then, Gandhi went much further than most in imagining the destruction of Westminster Abbey and the Houses of Parliament in London, shedding tears in the presence of the Viceroy at the thought of such an eventuality.[16] Naturally these tears were taken as a display of hypocrisy, and went on to become the subject of numerous jokes by the Mahatma's enemies. Even more outrageous were considered Gandhi's statements that Britain could not represent her struggle with fascism as being dedicated to the cause of freedom so long as she held countries like India in subjection, arguing that the British were only able to fight Nazism by adopting its violence. But if leaders like Churchill were mobilizing their people to die in the cause of liberty, why not train them to do so in a nonviolent way that might for the first time disrupt the never-ending cycle of military preparations and war? Only prejudice, thought Gandhi, could lead men to approve the first and reject the second way of sacrifice, since both demonstrated that men could indeed be made to give their lives in the cause of an ideal.

Instead of embarking upon the contradictory task of rejecting fascist violence by trying to match its ferocity, the Mahatma advised the British to prove their principled opposition to Nazism by letting Hitler's forces enter their country without a fight, while at the same time refusing to cooperate with them in any way. In the absence of armed opposition, he suggested, German troops would lose their purpose, and the refusal of civilians to cooperate with them would render Nazi rule impossible. But more than this it would display the kind of individual and everyday courage that were alone capable of converting Hitler's soldiers to the path of virtue. Only such a course of action, thought the Mahatma, could translate into reality the anti-fascist resolve that Britain was trumpeting to the world in the name of her people. Before dismissing this advice as unrealistic, we should recognize that the Mahatma never expected his counsel to be followed. He was simply making the argument that Britain's preparations for war were prompted by fear rather than courage, since they relied upon propaganda that demonized the Germans. Instead of creating in the war an exceptional situation where fear and hatred could flourish, therefore, Gandhi recommended dealing with fascism in the most quotidian of ways by refusing to suspend the moral norms of civilian life:

You want to kill Nazism. You will never kill it by its indifferent adoption. Your soldiers are doing the same work of destruction as the Germans. The only difference is that perhaps yours are not as thorough as the Germans. If that be so, yours will soon acquire the same thoroughness as theirs, if not much greater. On no other condition can you win the war. In other words, you will have to be more ruthless than the Nazis. No cause, however just, can warrant the indiscriminate slaughter that is going on minute by minute. I suggest that a cause that demands the inhumanities that are being perpetrated today cannot be called just. [...]

I venture to present you with a nobler and a braver way, worthy of the bravest soldier. I want you to fight Nazism without arms, or, if I am to retain the military terminology, with non-violent arms. I would like you to lay down the arms you have as being useless for saving you or humanity. You will invite Herr Hitler and Signor Mussolini to take what they want of the countries you call your possessions. Let them take possession of your beautiful island, with your many beautiful buildings. You will give all these, but neither your souls, nor your minds. If these gentlemen choose to occupy your homes, you will vacate them. If they do not give you free passage out, you will allow yourself, man, woman and child, to be slaughtered, but you will refuse to owe allegiance to them.[17]

By insisting upon dealing with fascism in the context of everyday life, of course, the Mahatma was voicing his support for morality as a universal enterprise, one that could not be shunted aside in the supposedly exceptional circumstances of war without losing its credibility. For he realized that allowing exceptions to the moral rule only ended up making morality itself into an exception, one whose limited scope was henceforth to be determined by the immorality of war. And the appeal to exceptional circumstances, Gandhi thought, was as likely to produce surrender as it did war, of which the "pragmatic" Czech non-resistance to German arms provided an unexceptionable instance. Morality, in other words, and nonviolence in particular, had to be effective even in the worst of circumstances if it was to retain validity, and indeed Gandhi thought that its form of resistance was practicable even when political resistance had become pointless, as was the case in Czechoslovakia. But for this to occur morality could not in effect depend upon immorality, as would be the case if it was conceived in negative terms merely as a method of resistance, and therefore itself an exceptional practice. On the contrary it had the positive duty of converting the enemy out of love for him. And if this Christian doctrine had in the past been used to justify violence, with the tortures of the Inquisition meant to destroy the sinner's body in order to save his soul, for Gandhi it entailed the general advocacy of nonviolence rather than the particular one of any creed.

Now for morality to become a universal enterprise of this kind, Hitler and his minions too had to be the objects of its love. Without minimizing what he called the evil of the Nazis in any way, therefore, the Mahatma felt bound to appeal to their sense of virtue even if no positive response was to be expected from it. Anything else would be to consign these men to the status of inhuman or subhuman beings, and thus inadvertently to join their evildoing by engaging in a politics of exceptionality. So in an article from his journal *Harijan*, Gandhi steadfastly refused to treat fascism as a moral exception and, like Iqbal and many other Indians, placed it on the same continuum as imperialism and even democracy:

They show in their family circles the same tenderness, affection, consideration and generosity that war-resisters are likely to show even outside such circles. The difference is only one of degree. Indeed Fascists and Nazis are a revised edition of so-called democracies if they are not an answer to the latter's misdeeds. [...] The so-called democracies have before now misappropriated other people's lands and have resorted to ruthless repression. What wonder if Messrs. Hitler and company have reduced to a science the unscientific violence their predecessors had developed for exploiting the so-called backward races for their own material gain?[18]

It is this view of fascism that allows us to account for the two letters Gandhi wrote Hitler, only the first of which was allowed to be published and sent to the *fuehrer* by British censors. Interesting about these letters is that they refer to shared ideals such as heroism and the love of one's people, with the Mahatma telling Hitler that these could most gloriously be fulfilled, and in historically the most unprecedented way, if he were to use his great power to advocate the cause of nonviolence, and suggesting therefore that the Nazis might take as an example of this India's struggle against their common enemy the British. At the same time, however, Gandhi made sure to inform the *fuehrer* that his violence was both unacceptable and simply a more scientific version of Britain's own, being equally incapable of withstanding

HITLER'S CONVERSION

nonviolent resistance, which refused to distinguish between war and peace. Here are some passages from the Mahatma's second letter to Hitler, dated 24 December 1940:

That I address you as a friend is no formality. I own no foes. [...] We have no doubt about your bravery or devotion to your fatherland, nor do we believe that you are the monster described by your opponents. But your own writings and pronouncements and those of your friends and admirers leave no room for doubt that many of your acts are monstrous and unbecoming of human dignity [...]. I am aware that your view of life regards such spoliations as virtuous acts. But we have been taught from childhood to regard them as acts degrading humanity. Hence we cannot possibly wish success to your arms.

But ours is a unique position. We resist British Imperialism no less than Nazism. If there is a difference, it is in degree. One-fifth of the human race has been brought under the British heel by means that will not bear scrutiny. Our resistance to it does not mean harm to the British people. We seek to convert them, not to defeat them on the battlefield. Ours is an unarmed revolt against the British rule. But whether we convert them or not, we are determined to make their rule impossible by non-violent non-co-operation. It is a method in its nature indefensible. It is based on the knowledge that no spoliator can compass his end without a certain degree of co-operation, willing or compulsory, of the victim. Our rulers may have our land and bodies but not our souls. They can have the former only by the complete destruction of every Indian—man, woman and child. That all may not rise to that degree of heroism and that a fair amount of frightfulness can bend the back of revolt is true but the argument would be beside the point. For, if a fair number of men and women be found in India who would be prepared without any ill will against the spoliators to lay down their lives rather than bend the knee to them, they would have shown the way to freedom from the tyranny of violence. [...]

We were groping for the right means to combat the most organized violence in the world which the British power represents. You have challenged it. It remains to be seen which is the better organized, the German or the British. We know what the British heel means for us and the non-European races of the world. But we would never wish to end British rule with German aid. We have found in non-violence a force which, if organized, can without doubt match itself against a combination of all the most violent forces in the world. In non-violent technique, as I have said, there is no such thing as defeat. It is all 'do or die' without killing or hurting. It can be used practically without money and obviously without the aid of the science of destruction which you have brought to such perfection. It is a marvel to me that you do not see that it is nobody's monopoly. If not the British, some other power will certainly improve upon your method and beat you with your own weapon. You are leaving no legacy to your people of which they would feel proud. They cannot take pride in a recital of cruel deeds, however skillfully planned. I, therefore, appeal to you in the name of humanity to stop the war.[19]

These appeals to Hitler were at best politically naïve, though Gandhi might have argued that they were also morally imperative, since he was interested not so much in the immediate task of preventing the spread of fascism, as in the long-term consequences of doing so both among the Nazis and their enemies. Thus his concern with converting fascists instead of merely defeating them, or with ensuring that anti-fascists did not lose their moral purpose in the struggle against Nazism. However tempting, it would be a mistake to see the Mahatma's concerns as being motivated by a superficial and sentimental attitude towards wrongdoing, not least because Gandhi had more experience than most with its darkest instances. Far from being an Indian Dr Pangloss, the Mahatma was as unsentimental a moralist as there could be, and from his earliest writings had recommended that the virtuous should make their hearts into "perfectly baked clay" impervious to emotions like hurt, fear and outrage.[20] Indeed he considered the passions of violence to be pumped-up products of sentiments like horror and pity that were perfectly virtuous in their own right, and held nonviolence to be not only the rational, but also inescapable conclusion of any ethics claiming universality for itself. It was the stoic impassiveness of this morality that was to receive its severest test in the controversy over Gandhi's advice to Germany's Jews, who were soon to face the Holocaust's unprecedented violence.

HITLER'S CONVERSION

Not the least important aspect of the Mahatma's articles and correspondence on the subject of Jews under Nazi rule is the fact that his abiding concern with this issue was unusual at the time, when anti-Semitism was yet to be seen as one of the most serious threats posed by fascism. His recommendations to them had as their background long-standing relations with Jewish friends and admirers, some of whom had been his staunchest supporters in South Africa. As an early celebrity of the international media, the Mahatma's advice was also sought by people from around the world, among them Jewish intellectuals such as Martin Büber and Judah Magnes.[21] Gandhi's own interest in the Jews had to do with their status as a minority, comparable in this respect to Indians in South Africa, to "Untouchables" in caste society (in a striking phrase he called the Jews the "Untouchables of Christianity"), to Hindus or Muslims in those parts of India where the other community formed a majority and to blacks in the United States. For the Mahatma thought that all moral action began with minorities, whether political, religious or racial, and furthermore considered their morality as being of the purest kind, precisely because it didn't have the sanction either of numbers or power. He even described the Czechs as a "minority" nation, saying that "what may ultimately prove impossible of acceptance by crores [millions] of people, undisciplined and unused till but recently to corporate suffering, might be possible for a small, compact, disciplined nation inured to corporate suffering".[22] Although they might be seduced from the paths of virtue as easily as any majority, therefore, for Gandhi minorities had a greater responsibility in upholding morality, and it was to remind the German Jews of their particular responsibility in combating fascism that he ventured to advise them.

European politics had been faced since at least the end of the First World War by the problem that minorities had come to pose for a post-imperial continent newly organized into nation states. Given that such states were rarely inhabited by single nations, however, minorities had come to possess a special juridical character in the League of Nations, which had the duty of protecting such groups against national majorities intent either on assimilating or dispensing with them. Despite the rather similar language of minority protection deployed by Muslims as well as Hindus in colonial India, Gandhi had no interest in identifying minorities of this sort primarily as victims, a category which in any case he thought possessed no moral standing whatever. At the same time as he lauded the contribution that Jews had made to the world's moral and cultural life in the highest terms, therefore, Gandhi refused to see any particular virtue in their historical suffering, describing Jewish endurance, however admirable it might otherwise be, merely as the nonviolence of the weak. More than this he responded to claims that the Jews were somehow sanctified in their suffering by pointing with disfavor to biblical conceptions of vengeance and to the "stigma" attached to them as Christ's killers, as if to say that even a history of immoral agency was preferable to one of victimization. Indeed Gandhi had always held that if nonviolent resistance was impossible, the undoubted evil of violence was preferable to such an acceptance, let alone a glorification of victimization. And this was the case because the acceptance of victimization, which Gandhi identified with cowardice, was more conducive to violence than violence itself. For the violence of self-defense, especially if it was doomed to failure, at least offered an opportunity for nonviolence by a demonstration of courage that was capable of satisfying the would-be victim's conscience as well as prompting the admiration of his assailant. "Between violence and cowardly flight, I can only prefer violence to cowardice. I can no more preach non-violence to a coward than I can tempt a blind man to enjoy healthy scenes".[23]

And it was because he maintained that only agents of one kind or another could be described as moral beings that the

HITLER'S CONVERSION

Mahatma insisted upon foregrounding the responsibility of minorities like the Jews, who should not allow themselves to become the passive victims of Nazism, and in doing so glorifying what he regarded as a wrong-headed sense of fortitude. But this they could only do by refusing to call for, and so depend upon, the armed intervention of Britain or America against Germany, which the Mahatma declared futile anyway, as states went to war out of national interest and not in order to protect others. This was the same advice Gandhi had given the Czechs, who could neither rely upon the help of the great powers nor fight Germany.[24] So in an article titled "The Jews" and published in *Harijan* on 26 November 1938, Gandhi acknowledged: "If there ever could be a justifiable war in the name of and for humanity, a war against Germany, to prevent the wanton persecution of a whole race, would be completely justified. But I do not believe in any war. A discussion of the pros and cons of such a war is therefore outside my horizon or province".[25] Claiming that as a minority they were better able to employ non-violent methods than the Czechs, he went on to recommend such a course of *satyagraha* to the Jews not because he thought this to be politically efficacious in the short term, but since he was concerned for their integrity as moral agents in the long run:

> If I were a Jew and were born in Germany and earned my livelihood there, I would claim Germany as my home even as the tallest gentile German may, and challenge him to shoot me or cast me in the dungeon; I would refuse to be expelled or to submit to discriminating treatment. And for doing this, I should not wait for the fellow Jews to join me in civil resistance but would have confidence that in the end the rest are bound to follow my example. If one Jew or all the Jews were to accept the prescription here offered, he or they cannot be worse off than they are now. And suffering voluntarily undergone will bring them an inner strength and joy which no number of resolutions of sympathy passed in the world outside Germany can. Indeed, even if Britain, France and America were to declare hostilities against Germany, they can bring no inner joy, no inner strength. The calculated vio-

lence of Hitler may even result in a general massacre of the Jews by way of his first answer to the declaration of such hostilities. But if the Jewish mind could be prepared for voluntary suffering, even the massacre I have imagined could be turned into a day of thanksgiving and joy that Jehovah had wrought deliverance of the race even at the hands of the tyrant.[26]

Though his Jewish correspondents denied being warmongers intent on persuading the great powers to act on their behalf, vehemently rejected any characterization of Judaism as a vengeful religion and even claimed to have been practicing nonviolence for some two thousand years, Gandhi had only said to them what he did to his own people, urging Hindus and Muslims not to rely upon the might of Britain in dealing with each other. And in this way he was yet again refusing to treat the evil of fascism as a moral exception, reacting to claims that he hadn't understood its uniqueness by pointing out that the legal and political position of Indians in South Africa, during his nonviolent struggle there, was comparable to that of Germany's Jews before the war. This was of course not entirely correct as far as the treatment of German Jews went, but then the Mahatma's argument had to do not so much with establishing an exact comparison between them and South Africa's Indians, as with denying the claim to uniqueness and exceptionality either for fascism or its victims on strictly moral grounds:

[In South Africa] the Indians occupied precisely the same place that the Jews occupy in Germany. The persecution had also a religious tinge. President Kruger used to say that the white Christians were the chosen of God and Indians were inferior beings created to serve the whites. A fundamental clause in the Transvaal constitution was that there should be no equality between the whites and colored races including Asiatics. There too the Indians were consigned to ghettos described as locations. The other disabilities were almost of the same type as those of the Jews in Germany. The Indians, a mere handful, resorted to satyagraha without any backing from the world outside or the Indian Government. Indeed the British officials tried to dissuade the satyagrahis from their contemplated step. World opinion and the Indian Government came to their aid after eight years of fighting. And that too was by way of diplomatic pressure not a threat of war.[27]

The Mahatma's warnings to the Jews regarding their dependence upon the might of others, especially of imperialist Britain, had a history going back to the end of the First World War, when he had told the Zionists that it was immoral to impose themselves on Palestine with the help of British bayonets. While he was not against Jewish settlement in Palestine, or even a Jewish state there, Gandhi thought this could only be achieved with Arab support, itself solicited by Zionist self-reliance in the attempt to create a political future for both peoples that had no precedent in the history of nations. The increasing popularity of Zionism among Jews in wartime Europe once again made their settlement in the Holy Land a political issue, and Gandhi engaged with it along the same lines as he had earlier.[28] Indeed given the concern of his Jewish correspondents with Zionism as much as fascism, the Mahatma dealt with both issues together. Thus he maintained that if their presence in the Holy Land was truly a religious obligation, then the Jews should wish only to visit it as pilgrims, and if they would settle there, could not do so as Palestine's rulers without violating this religious sanction. In the same article he went so far as to state that by seeking to displace the Arabs the Zionists were doing nothing more than providing a "colorable" justification for the admittedly harsher German attempts to eliminate European Jewry in order to achieve a national home and *lebensraum* for themselves. While Gandhi's Zionist correspondents denied such arguments repeatedly, he held fast to them as in the following passage:

And now a word to the Jews in Palestine. I have no doubt that they are going about it in the wrong way. The Palestine of the Biblical conception is not a geographical tract. It is in their hearts. But if they must look to the Palestine of geography as their national home, it is wrong to enter it under the shadow of the British gun. A religious act cannot be performed with the aid of the bayonet or the bomb. They can settle in Palestine only by the goodwill of the Arabs. They should seek to convert the Arab heart. The same God rules the Arab heart who rules the Jewish heart. They can offer satyagraha in front of the Arabs and offer themselves to be shot or thrown into the Dead Sea without raising a little finger against them. They will find the world opinion in their favor in their religious aspiration. There are hundreds of ways of reasoning with the Arabs, if they will only discard the help of the British bayonet. As it is, they are co-sharers with the British in despoiling a people who have done no wrong to them.[29]

Although he was told by more than one of his Jewish correspondents that Zionism did not necessarily involve a religious aspiration, Gandhi insisted on describing its virtue in religious terms alone, perhaps because he realized that only such an aspiration could sanction the kind of action he called for and make for a set of moral relations between Arabs and Jews that a merely territorial claim on Palestine could not. As it is, many of his Zionist interlocutors justified their claims by reference to the same language of improvement and civilization that European colonialism deployed in places like India, representing therefore the kind of morality that the Mahatma was unable to accept. And this was of course the same position he adopted towards Muslim separatism in India, whose claim that Pakistan, as a state in which a minority dispersed throughout the Subcontinent could become a nation, was based on similar principles which in his opinion lacked the moral integrity that a truly religious aspiration might give it. The problem with both Jewish and Muslim politics was therefore its inability to create moral relationships with others, being doomed to deal with them in the idiom of violence alone. Naturally those who opposed these movements were not blameless when it came to such violence, but Gandhi thought that setting a moral example was primarily the responsibility of Muslim and Jewish nationalists, who were after all dedicated to the establishment of new societies rather than submitting to the regulations of an old one.

HITLER'S CONVERSION

Politics beside itself

Not surprisingly, the easiest and apparently most convincing way of objecting to Gandhi's recommendations was to describe them as unrealistic. But in a shrewd comment from an article published in *Harijan* on 17 December 1938, in which he responded to a letter from one of the Germans objecting to his piece on "The Jews" a month before, Gandhi saw in the very violence with which his recommendations were dismissed an uneasy recognition of their merit: "It passes comprehension why any German should be angry over my utterly innocuous writing. Of course, German critics, as others, might have ridiculed it by saying that it was a visionary's effort doomed to fail. I therefore welcome this wrath, though wholly unmerited, against my writing. Has my writing gone home? Has the writer felt that my remedy was after all not so ludicrous as it may appear, but that it was eminently practical if only the beauty of suffering without retaliation was realized?"[30] Going further in another article published in the same issue of *Harijan*, Gandhi made it clear that nonviolent resistance could not be dismissed as being unworkable at a mass level, prejudicial to military efforts at saving the Jews or indeed as being a failure in India itself:

Of course, the critics can reasonably argue that the non-violence pictured by me is not possible for masses of mankind. It is possible only for the very few highly developed persons. I have combated that view and suggested that, given proper training and proper generalship, non-violence can be practiced by masses of mankind.

I see, however, that my remarks are being misunderstood to mean that because I advise non-violent resistance by the persecuted Jews, by inference I expect or would advise non-interference by the democratic Powers on behalf of the Jews. I hardly need to answer this fear. Surely there is no danger of the great Powers refraining from action because of anything I have said. They will, they are bound to, do all they can to free the Jews from the inhuman persecution. My appeal has force in the face of the fact that the great Powers feel unable to help the Jews in an effective manner. Therefore it is that I have offered the prescription which I know to be infallible when taken in the right manner.

The most relevant criticism, however, which I have received is this: How do I expect the Jews to accept my prescription when I know that India, where I am myself working, where I call myself the self-appointed general, has not accepted it in toto. My answer is: "Blessed are they that expect nothing". I belong to the category of the blessed, in this case at least. Having got the prescription and being sure of its efficacy, I felt that I would be wrong if I did not draw attention to it when I saw cases where it could be effectively applied.[31]

The Mahatma also refuted such accusations of "idealism" by claiming that his advice could be put into effect immediately by any German Jew, and was therefore far more realistic, as well as being morally meaningful at an individual level, than the lengthy and uncertain endeavors of Jewish elites in Britain or America to enlist the assistance of their governments in stopping Nazi violence. Rather than trying merely to avert fascism's murderous logic by in effect countering it with an alternative form of state violence, Gandhi suggested that Nazism's complete and comprehensive defeat had to be accomplished by private individuals, and in doing so inverted the logic of conventional politics, which accorded this privilege to states alone. This is what the Mahatma had always advised Indians fighting imperialism, who like the Jews were told they might accomplish their aim in a way that no state or army ever could if they displayed the requisite spirit of nonviolence and self-sacrifice. Only in this way could they hope to convert the votaries of hatred and violence by the force of their example. For nonviolence was in the end not an ideal but an everyday reality upon which all societies depended well beyond any guarantee provided by the law: "I hold that non-violence is not merely a personal virtue. It is also a social virtue to be cultivated like other virtues. Surely society is largely regulated by the expression of non-violence in its mutual dealings. What I ask for is an extension of it on a larger, national and international scale".[32]

HITLER'S CONVERSION

Available even to the weakest and most oppressed individuals, such a course of action entailed engaging with those ideals that the Nazis shared with the rest of humankind, and laying claim to them in a manner that showed these victims to be their truest agents. The presence of such ideals not only humanized each party in the eyes of the other, while at the same time allowing the engagement of virtue with vice to remain morally uncompromised, but it also bore witness to one of Gandhi's most important doctrines, that evil too depended upon goodness and so possessed no integrity of its own.[33] By this the Mahatma meant that even the most brutal forms of domination necessarily relied upon the loyalty, friendship and selflessness of its supporters, whether or not they had been duped into upholding these virtues. Such allies, after all, could not be motivated simply by fear, hatred or self-interest if they were willing to die for the cause they espoused, one that would collapse immediately in the absence of such virtues. But this implied that evil was unable in the final instance to control even its own instruments, who were guided by a goodness that might be perverted but never extinguished. The task of nonviolent resistance, then, was to expose evil's precarious position and draw support away from it by appealing to its own virtues, in this case by the Jews claiming through their acts of nonviolent resistance to be the truest of Germans. So in his article on "The Jews", Gandhi made the point that rather than being worse off than the Indians in South Africa who had deployed nonviolent resistance against the state, the Jews of Germany were actually in a better position to make use of it in claiming that country's virtues for themselves:

But the Jews of Germany can offer satyagraha under infinitely better auspices than the Indians of South Africa. The Jews are a compact, homogeneous community in Germany. They are far more gifted than the Indians of South Africa. And they have organized world opinion behind them. I am convinced that if someone with courage and vision can arise among them to lead them in non-violent action, the winter of their despair can in the twinkling of an eye be turned into the summer of hope. And what has today become a degrading man-hunt can be turned into a calm and determined stand offered by unarmed men and women possessing the strength of suffering given to them by Jehovah. It will be then a truly religious resistance offered against the godless fury of dehumanized man. The German Jews will score a lasting victory over the German gentiles in the sense that they will have converted the latter to an appreciation of human dignity. They will have rendered service to fellow-Germans and proved their title to be the real Germans, as against those who are today dragging, however unknowingly, the German name into the mire.[34]

When in an editorial *The Statesman* of London ridiculed Gandhi's opinion that the courage of suffering voluntarily undergone had the ability to convert fascists, pointing to the apparently useless suffering of such courageous men as Pastor Niemoeller at the hands of the Nazis, he responded in an article on 7 January 1939, saying that suffering was never in vain, for though it might not save lives in the present its consequences in the future were assured. In other words this kind of "pointless" resistance not only safeguarded the moral integrity of its agent in the present, it also laid the groundwork for evil's conversion in the future, if only by offering Germans in times to come an example of courage different from that of Nazism, and one with which they could identify and thus be converted. In opposition to *The Statesman*, he also pointed out that the apparently useless suffering of Jesus possessed the most significant political consequences:

I do not think that the sufferings of Pastor Niemoeller and others have been in vain. They have preserved their self-respect intact. They have proved that their faith was equal to any suffering. That they have not proved sufficient for melting Herr Hitler's heart merely shows that it is made of a harder material than stone. [...] Herr Hitler is but one man enjoying no more than the average span of life. He would be a spent force if he had not the backing of his people. I do not despair of his responding to human suffering even though caused by him. But I must refuse to believe that the Germans as a nation have no heart or markedly less than the other nations of the earth. They will some day or other rebel against their own adored hero,

HITLER'S CONVERSION

if he does not wake up betimes. And when he or they do, we shall find that the sufferings of the Pastor and his fellow-workers had not a little to do with the awakening. [...] I was unprepared to find the view expressed by *The Statesman*'s writer that the example of Christ proved once and for all that in a worldly and temporal sense it can fail hopelessly!![35]

While Gandhi's critics were focused exclusively on short-term solutions to the evil of fascism, and therefore favored a politics calibrated in many respects to the exceptionality they recognized in Nazism, the Mahatma entertained a rather different view of the situation. To begin with he refused to see it as exceptional, thus the comparisons drawn with imperialism, described not as the more authentic exception, but rather as yet another illustration of moral perversion. Only by naturalizing fascism in this way could Gandhi maintain the moral universality of *ahimsa*, or nonviolence, something that had to be practiced in the same way whatever the conditions involved. Indeed we have already seen how Gandhi tried to turn military conditions into civilian ones by recommending that the British allow Hitler's armies into their country and resist them nonviolently. And unlike his interlocutors, who while accusing the Mahatma of sentimentalism and priding themselves on hard headed political judgment, were in fact entirely consumed by the horror of the moment, Gandhi was willing to look at the situation in the long term. Very much like the "realist" politicians who led the battle against Nazism, he was capable of tolerating any number of deaths in the present to secure fascism's defeat, if only at the hands of a virtue untainted by it. Here, for example, is a fragment from his response to a lengthy article published by Hayim Greenberg in the *Jewish Frontier* of March 1939 under the title "An Answer to Gandhi":

It is highly probable that, as the writer says, "a Jewish Gandhi in Germany, should one arise, could function for about five minutes and would be promptly taken to the guillotine". But that will not disprove my case or shake my belief in the efficacy of ahimsa. I can conceive the necessity of the immolation of hundreds, if not thousands, to appease the hunger of dictators who have no belief in ahimsa. Indeed the maxim is that ahimsa is the most efficacious in front of the greatest himsa [violence]. Its quality is really tested only in such cases. Sufferers need not see the result during their lifetime. They must have faith that if their cult survives, the result is a certainty. The method of violence gives no greater guarantee than that of non-violence. It gives infinitely less. For the faith of the votary of ahimsa is lacking.[36]

Had they not been so keen to see him as a sentimental and idealistic figure, the Mahatma's critics would have noticed that he was in some sense as hard-hearted as Hitler where human suffering was concerned. For as long as it was voluntarily undergone, this suffering could only receive Gandhi's approbation as a form of heroism, while those who suffered only as victims enjoyed no moral standing in his eyes. Had he known about it, the Mahatma would undoubtedly have pointed to the Warsaw Ghetto uprising of 1943 as an illustration of his teaching. For this struggle was dedicated not to the victory or even survival of those Jews trapped in Warsaw who resisted the German armed forces in an unequal battle, but rather to "the honor and glory of the Jewish people", words that formed the uprising's motto in defiance of all political calculation.[37] Though he was opposed to needless suffering, therefore, Gandhi saw enough virtue in its voluntary form to justify the death of thousands for moral reasons. His idea of morality, in other words, did not take life as its end, departing in this way from conventional politics, in which one life could only be taken to protect another. Indeed the sovereignty of modern states is predicated upon the ability to preserve the lives of citizens, if only by requiring their sacrifice from time to time, to say nothing about the sacrifice of enemy lives.

But if the giving, taking, improvement and general management of life defines the very purpose of politics, including and especially that of Nazism with its cult of biological purity, can the Mahatma's refusal to base his morality on the preservation of life be seen as anti-political in nature? For however radically it might have departed from European politics in other respects, Nazism was conventional in its desire to uphold some forms of human life against others, differing only in its demarcation of such life forms and the methods by which they were to be protected. The priority he gave virtue led Gandhi to display a certain lack of concern with death and defeat as political facts, yet he never propagated such virtuous actions purely for their own sake. In fact they were meant to have consequences of a very practical or life-affirming kind, and Gandhi even saw morality as providing among all human actions the only guaranteed outcome. Politics, on the other hand, despite being defined in his view by pure instrumentality in the service of race or class, country or empire, was generally unable to fulfill even its own ends. And as we have seen in the previous chapter from Gandhi's commentary on the *Gita*, this was due to the fact that while it depended upon creating a future by a calculus of cause and effect, politics could never fully control its means and was therefore doomed to uncertainty and incompletion.

The guaranteed consequences of moral action, however, required time and suffering to manifest themselves, though not in the way in which the sacrifice of the few for the many, or the present for the future, was conceptualized in the language of politics. For one thing the Mahatma saw in sacrifice the means of establishing a moral relationship between enemies rather than with friends who required saving. And for another he did not glorify death in one place because it made life possible in another, holding instead that the consequences of suffering and death were dictated not by political instrumentality but moral action, whose principles remained the same in times of war and peace alike. And in this way Gandhi tried to subordinate politics to morality by depriving the former of autonomy, in effect saying that its aims could only be achieved in virtue practiced according to a rather different set of rules, almost as a kind of miracle foretold. In other words he had turned the outcomes to which politics is dedicated into a set of expected yet unplanned demonstrations of divine grace, thus removing them from the realm of human instrumentality. But to do this Gandhi had to separate morality from life, seen as the very principle of politics, and thus tolerate the suffering, death and even extinction of entire peoples in the name of nonviolence. In the passage from his response to the *Jewish Frontier* quoted above, for example, the Mahatma is willing to contemplate the elimination of the Jews as a people in the path of virtue, while at the same time arguing that nonviolent resistance was capable of achieving their political salvation more effectively than any war could. This double logic, in which one statement runs alongside another without the two ever meeting, illustrates the way in which Gandhi tried to subject politics to morality, a course of action he adopted throughout his career. The severity of his moral recommendations, in other words, was always matched by the promise of political liberation, something that the Mahatma's critics thought hypocritical in the extreme.

Whether or not he was a hypocrite, the Mahatma's declared aim of spiritualizing politics had to do with demonstrating that its ends might be achieved more effectively by a quite different set of principles. And for this time was of the essence, not only making possible the enemy's conversion through a display of voluntary suffering, but doing so by abandoning all the instruments of politics, from violence to victory, so as to make of temporality the site of divine grace rather than human purpose. When speaking to Indian audiences, the Mahatma often described such time in messianic terms, as a site for God's incarnation, something that prayer and moral action could call upon but never create. Responding to a Dutchman who had written him about the dehumanizing brutalities of Nazism, Gandhi pointed out that whereas political action was always limited by a faith in some outcome within the bounds of probability, and was so unable to take any risks despite its tendency to fail, moral activity attempted the impossible and was thus capable of changing the parameters of probability, demonstrations of which he frequently said were recounted by the history of religious movements. As long as its results could be neither planned nor foreseen by political calculation, then, such action might be said to be divine in nature:

> The British Government can take no risks, can make no experiments in which they have not even a workable faith. But if ever an opportunity could be given to me, in spite of my physical limitations, I should not hesitate to try what would appear to be impossible. For in ahimsa it is not the votary who acts in his own strength. Strength comes from God. If, therefore, the way is opened for me to go, he will give me the physical endurance and clothe my word with the needed power. Anyway all through my life I have acted in that faith. Never have I attributed my independent strength to myself. This may be considered by men who do not believe in a higher power than themselves as a drawback and a helpless state. I must admit that limitation of ahimsa, if it be accounted as such.[38]

The time of suffering, in other words, could not be politically instrumental because it involved the deliberate negation of life as a principle of action and so laid itself open to other ways of conceiving agency. And yet it was this very renunciation of politics that allowed for the fulfillment of its objectives. No amount of fascist brutality, therefore, was capable of shaking Gandhi's belief in nonviolence, as long as there was time to suffer, and he refused to believe that the Nazis could conceal such suffering from ordinary Germans by spiriting away their opponents in the middle of the night. But what if time was lacking for the manifestation of moral as much as political agency? Never asked during the course of the war in Europe, this question came to haunt the Mahatma in the aftermath of the bombing of Hiroshima and Nagasaki. After all, nuclear weapons ensured the defeat of a population in an instant, giving them no time to resist nonviolently. The atom bomb, moreover, separated assailants from victims by such a distance as to nullify any such display and the moral relations it sought to create between violence and nonviolence. Here was the first serious challenge posed to nonviolence as a theory of action, and one that came not from fascism in its own right, but by way of those who had fought it only to discover a means of violence greater than any deployed by their enemies. It was as if Gandhi's prediction, that matching violence with violence would only increase its power, had finally come true in the most fearsome way.

Not fascism, then, but its defeat posed the greatest challenge to the Mahatma's belief in the universal applicability of nonviolence. Indeed the unprecedented future that was inaugurated by the bombing of Hiroshima and Nagasaki seemed to have shocked Gandhi so profoundly as to leave him silent on the subject for some time. He had of course always been critical of modern technology, which allowed men to dispense with each other's labor while marking their distance from the moral relations by which local communities functioned, but the bomb represented something more than an increase in speed or a decrease in time. Its violence appeared to have rendered suffering meaningless not only in a practical sense, illustrated by the conversion of an enemy or at least the transformation of his political strategy, but also by denying it a role in the making of a moral subject. This had not been the case even with the aerial bombardment preceding the deployment of atomic weapons, which did not preclude more intimate forms of combat, and still preserved some interaction between similarly armed enemies. So what meaning could sacrifice possess in a nuclear war where, as in the Cold War doctrine of Mutually Assured Destruction, neither winners nor losers might survive? This was a question as important for politics as it was for morality, and one for which no answer has yet been proffered.[39] After all if winning had become in some sense equivalent to losing, and the fate of the human race as such was put into question by a nuclear war, then what meaning could sacrifice or suffering possess?

In the end Gandhi could only say that if people who were targeted by nuclear weapons refused not only to fight but also take shelter in bunkers, this would at least demonstrate that they were moral agents rather than hapless victims, capable of dying fearlessly and in doing so vindicating their honor, something he saw as being morally as well as politically more precious than life. Indeed this courage was alone capable of converting their enemies, even if only in times to come, while also ensuring that such of their descendants who survived would look upon this collective death with pride rather than be consumed by the kind of humiliation and rage that led only to more violence.[40] We have already seen the Mahatma deploy similar arguments in his advice to the Jews, but whereas he predicted that moral action could bring about a political outcome during their lifetime, the possibility of nuclear annihilation forced him to make such a result entirely posthumous. And so the nonviolent resistance of those who died in an atomic war lost its remaining political consequences to become a pure act of moral agency, whose task was to offer both enemies and friends the possibility of redemption in an undefined future.

Gandhi thus converted the war's ostensible victims into agents capable of redeeming those who had managed to survive it, in a striking reversal that was deeply religious while retaining at the same time some political meaning despite itself. Indeed the morality of nonviolence might even be seen as the last redoubt of a politics that had lost its own character. For the atom bomb, by representing either the absolute power of its owners over all others, or the paralysis and mutual annihilation of those who possessed it, had in some sense rendered politics impossible in the kind of war it presaged. Politics, therefore, suddenly took the place of morality as an exception confined to life conducted in the shadow of nuclear war, which in its turn could only be dealt with by strictly moral action if it was to admit of any consequences beyond nihilism. Or as the Mahatma put it when asked in an interview if the atom bomb had not rendered nonviolence meaningless: "No. It is the only thing the atom bomb cannot destroy. I did not move a muscle when I first heard that the atom bomb had wiped out Hiroshima. On the contrary, I said to myself, 'unless now the world adopts non-violence, it will spell certain suicide for mankind'".[41] In other words, while a politics dedicated to the preservation of life had proven its hollowness by placing humanity itself under threat, the morality of nonviolence had made such life possible by disregarding it altogether. And so the vindication that fascism's potential victory could not give Gandhi's theory of nonviolence was in this paradoxical way assured by its defeat.

6

LEAVING INDIA TO ANARCHY

During the last great agitation he launched against colonial rule, the Quit India Movement of 1942, Gandhi accused the British of having become a hindrance to India's political development and asked them to leave the country to God or anarchy. Made as it was in the middle of the Second World War, this demand would in effect have compelled Britain to abandon India to a possible Japanese invasion, and so it was chiefly as an attempt to sabotage the war effort that the Quit India Movement was judged, with the Indian National Congress seen as blackmailing the government in this way to concede more power to it. But in a context where India's major political parties could not come to any agreement about a future constitution for the country, the Mahatma's demand was also interpreted as an effort on the part of the biggest among them to bulldoze its way to power by the threat of civil disobedience. And this meant that India's second largest party, the Muslim League, viewed itself as the movement's target as much as did the colonial government, with which it therefore hastened to ally itself for the duration of the war.

Since Gandhi was partial to anarchy as much as he was devoted to God, we should perhaps recognize in his demand that the British leave India to God or anarchy a literal rather than metaphorical desire. For even in the early days of his political and spiritual career, the Mahatma had struggled to rescue the anarchism of those who feared only God and were thus willing to risk disorder in upholding the truth, from that represented by terrorists who spread anarchy out of purely worldly and so immoral fears having to do with foreign or indeed any other kind of domination. Such an immoral anarchism, he suggested, could bring itself to fear anyone and anything, perhaps even the Indian people themselves, who the terrorists seemed to think were content to live as slaves and thus required the shock of violence to inspire in them the desire for freedom. So in a famous speech from 1916 he had this to say about the link between God, fear and anarchy:

We may foam, we may fret, we may resent but let us not forget that the India of to-day in her impatience has produced an army of anarchists. I am myself an anarchist, but of another type. But there is a class of anarchists amongst us, and if I was able to reach this class, I would say to them that their anarchism has no room in India if India is to conquer the conqueror. It is a sign of fear. If we trust and fear God, we shall have to fear no one, not Maharajahs, not Viceroys, not the detectives, not even King George.[1]

But whatever his previous relations with the deity or anarchism, Gandhi's demand that the British leave India to God or anarchy represented an attack on the moral basis of their rule, which at this time consisted in protecting India from the ravages of war on the one hand, and maintaining law and order in a situation where political disagreements among Indians prevented power being transferred to them on the other. Indeed the words of advice that India's penultimate viceroy, Lord Wavell, received from his predecessor Lord Linlithgow in 1942, dealt precisely with the question of Britain's responsibility to India and so the world at large:

He spoke at length of the possibilities of the political situation, at my request. He showed me Gandhi's final letter to him and his reply. He does not believe any real progress is possible while G. lives, and believes we shall have to continue responsibility for India for at least another 30 years. We could not for the peace of the world allow chaos in India. [...] He said the problem of removing British control from India was that of getting a three legged stool (Hindu, Moslem, British) to remain stable with one leg removed. [...] He said that we must be careful that we did not get into a position where we could not get out of India because of the chaos it would cause but were unable to control and administer it if we remained.[2]

Though he might easily have questioned the sincerity of such commitments, which, after all, appeared to provide Britain with convenient reasons for continuing her rule over India, the Mahatma did not spend much time doing so and was concerned instead with attacking their self-proclaimed morality. And it is important to note here that far from constituting examples of some long discarded imperialism, such commitments are no less central to justifications of occupation today. For even those who condemn certain forms of military intervention in foreign countries will often approve of others, as long as they are convincingly dedicated to saving lives or establishing law and order, and in this way expanding the arena of their political responsibility to the ends of the earth.

Yet it was precisely the commitment to save lives and preserve order that Gandhi questioned in 1942, and he did so not in order to defend principles like sovereignty and non-interference, as realists do in the field of international relations today, but so as to reject its moral basis. Being concerned about the consequences of their actions, he seemed to think, inflated Britain's claims of responsibility to such a degree as to deprive her politics of autonomy and meaning, thus robbing this much-vaunted responsibility of any reality. We have already seen in a previous chapter that for Gandhi morality consisted rather in escaping the never-ending process of cause and effect symbolized in the cycle of rebirth, and by refusing to take responsibility for all the consequences of one's actions, to shatter the gigantic system of determinations that made meaningful action impossible. Ultimately it was the expansion of responsibility and not its diminution that defined the nature of imperialism, whose concern for consequences forced it to rule out options like departure while being unable to propose any politics of a more imaginative kind in its place. It was to break this deadlock and make an imaginative politics possible that the Mahatma asked the British to quit India. But he did not stop at asking Britain to recognize the limits of her responsibility by leaving India to God or anarchy. For Gandhi also added that the disorder resulting from such a withdrawal was to be prized in its own right. And it is the logic and implications of such an apparently outrageous claim that I mean to explore in this chapter.

For an irresponsible politics

Faced with accusations that by launching a campaign asking the British to leave India precipitately he wanted to impede the war's successful conclusion, or even that he favoured a Japanese victory, Gandhi responded by suggesting that a free India might well continue to prosecute the war and agree to Allied troops being stationed on her territory. More than this, he maintained that an India liberated would better be able to contribute to the war effort, for then she would be fighting voluntarily and for her own sake. But in bondage Indians were capable of sympathizing with Japan instead, which was viewed by some among them as an Asian power fighting a common European enemy:

India is not playing any effective part in the War. Some of us feel ashamed that it is so and, what is more, we feel that if we were free from the foreign yoke, we should play a worthy, nay, a decisive part in the World War which has yet to reach its climax. We know that if India does not become free *now*, the hidden discontent will burst forth into a welcome to the Japanese, should they effect a landing. We feel that such an event would be a calamity of the first magnitude. We can avoid it if India gains her freedom.[3]

LEAVING INDIA TO ANARCHY

Given the recruitment of captured Indian troops by the German and Japanese armies, British authorities could be forgiven for regarding such statements as piously formulated threats. However the loyalty displayed by the vast majority of Indian soldiers during the war, and the lack of support that the landing eventually attempted by the Japanese and their turncoat troops received, demonstrated the unreality of this supposed threat. But as we might expect, Gandhi did not merely offer collaboration with the enemy as an alternative to a free India playing her rightful role in the war. Instead of being grateful for British protection and the peace that statesmen like Churchill claimed it had given her for well over a century, the Mahatma argued that India was being morally enfeebled by the very safety of her slavery, and longed for his compatriots to experience the full horror of war as the nations of Europe did, which was why he refused to wait for the end of the World War to make his demand:

> It is not open to them to say that we must smother our consciences and say or do nothing because there is war. That is why I have made up my mind that it would be a good thing if a million people were shot in a brave and non-violent rebellion against British rule. It may be that it may take us years before we can evolve order out of chaos. But we can then face the world. We cannot face the world today. Avowedly the different nations are fighting for their liberty. Germany, Japan, Russia, China are pouring their blood and money like water. What is *our* record? [...] We are betraying a woeful cowardice. I do not mind the blood-bath in which Europe is plunged. It is bad enough, but there is a great deal of heroism—mothers losing their only children, wives their husbands and so on.[4]

Having in his usual fashion refused to distinguish war from peace as far as the practice of morality was concerned, the Mahatma went further in refusing to distinguish between the struggles for freedom that he thought all parties to the war were engaged in by 1942. His only wish was for India to join this struggle and in doing so redeem her capacity for moral action. This kind of reasoning beggared belief, at least among Gandhi's enemies, who were compelled to adjudge him a consummate hypocrite if not a madman. Yet noteworthy about such reasoning is the care with which it sought to void the British justification for ruling India of any moral sanction, and this not by accusing its upholders of the hypocrisy they so freely attributed him, but instead by denying even the theoretical virtue claimed by such justifications. And this absolute negation, let us remember, was directed not simply at the disingenuous arguments of a colonial power bent on continuing her rule, but rather at the concept of political responsibility as we understand it today. It was therefore quite irrelevant if British policy in India happened to be disingenuous, self-deluding or on the contrary genuine and well intentioned.

Apart from the exigencies of war, the main reason why Gandhi's demand for Britain to quit India was considered unrealistic had to do with the fact that its people were too weak and divided to have power thrust upon them so suddenly. But it was Britain's very inability to transfer power to a politically unified nation that made the Mahatma call for her immediate withdrawal, for it was only in so doing, paradoxically, that she could claim to have acted for moral reasons alone:

> The novelty of the demand should not be missed. It is a demand not for a transference of power from Great Britain to a free India. For there is no party to which Britain would transfer such power. We lack the unity that gives strength. The demand therefore is not based on our demonstrable strength. It is a demand made upon Britain to do the right irrespective of the capacity of the party wronged to bear the consequences of Britain's right act. Will Britain restore seized property to the victim merely because the seizure was wrong? It is none of her concern to weigh whether the victim will be able to hold possession of the restored property. Hence it is that I have been obliged to make use of the word anarchy in this connection. This great moral act must give Britain moral status which should ensure victory. Whether without India Britain would have any reason to fight is a question I need not consider.[5]

LEAVING INDIA TO ANARCHY

If by quitting her Indian empire Britain would win the war, or be deprived of her reason of fighting it against Japan at least, such an action would also in Gandhi's view transform the political situation in India so as to allow for a settlement between its various parties, which he thought the colonial power's mere presence had until then prevented. And so by asking them to leave, the Mahatma was in effect demanding of the British nothing more than that they should follow his own example, by withdrawing cooperation from an evil situation so as to transform its conditions of possibility. This was why Britain's departure, in violation of all the norms of political responsibility, had to occur in the absence of negotiations and settlements, which could only take place among Indians themselves after her withdrawal:

> But the point I want to stress is this, *viz.*, that there is no room left for negotiations in the proposal for withdrawal. Either they recognize independence or they don't. After that recognition many things can follow. For by that one single act the British representatives will have altered the face of the whole landscape and revived the hope of the people which has been frustrated times without number. [...] But your next legitimate question would be—'How will free India function?' And because there was that knot, I said 'Leave India to God or anarchy'. But in practice what will happen is this—if withdrawal takes place in perfect goodwill, the change will be effected without the slightest disturbance. People would have to come to their own without disturbance. Wise people from among the responsible sections will come together and will evolve a Provisional Government. Then there will be no anarchy, no interruption, and a crowning glory. [...] But I am clear that it won't be a party government. All parties—including the Congress—will automatically dissolve. Of course other parties may come into being afterwards.[6]

Only a British withdrawal, in other words, would force India's various parties to come to an agreement by engaging in direct negotiations with one another on the basis of their own strength, rather than dealing which each other indirectly by a politics of pressures applied and promises offered the colonial state. But in the absence of this third party, said Gandhi, "That party or a combination which takes over control of India will have to look to the remaining parties for its retention of power. There is no hope of the parties coming together so long as they have to look not to one another but to an outsider for support and sustenance".[7] Now the British, of course, were unwilling to compromise their notions of political responsibility by abandoning India to chaos, though the settlement they eventually negotiated when leaving in 1947 arguably resulted in the very anarchy they had sought to avoid. Even more appalled by the Mahatma's reasoning, however, were India's smaller parties, and chief among them the Muslim League, whose leaders saw in it nothing more than an ill-conceived attempt on the part of Congress to expel the colonial power in order to crush them under the heel of an absolute Hindu majority. Naturally Gandhi not only denied this intention, he also maintained that even if true it was incapable of fulfilment, given the sheer size of the Muslim population and the fragmentation of Hindu society, which had after all been dominated for centuries by minorities like the Muslims themselves before the British took their place.[8] But the Muslim League, which saw in the fate of Hinduism's enormous population of low castes a portent of its people's future, was not to be persuaded by such arguments. When dealing with the fears of his Muslim correspondents, therefore, the Mahatma coupled his assurances of impartial treatment for all Indians with a startlingly open vision of India's future without Britain:

What will happen after, if ever we reach that stage, will depend upon how we act when the all-powerful British hand is withdrawn. We may quarrel among ourselves or we may adjust our quarrels and agree to set up ordered rule on behalf of the people. It may be a democratic constitution or an unadulterated autocracy or oligarchy. The conception is not that of a settlement with the British Government. That could happen only if there is a settlement between the principal parties, and as a preliminary the Congress and the League. But that so far as I see is not to be.

LEAVING INDIA TO ANARCHY

Therefore the only settlement with the British Government can be that their rule should end leaving India to her fate. Thus assuming that the British leave, there is no government and no constitution, British or other. Therefore there is no Central Government. Militarily the most powerful party may set up its rule and impose it on India if the people submit. Muslims may declare Pakistan and nobody may resist them. Hindus may do likewise, Sikhs may set up their rule in territories inhabited by them. There is no end to the possibilities. And to all this idle speculation let me suggest one more addition. The Congress and the League being the best organized parties in the country may come to terms and set up a provisional government acceptable to all.[9]

The chaos that might result from Britain's precipitate departure, Gandhi suggested, was preferable to the armed peace that existed, not least because it offered the possibility of a new and imaginative politics emerging to address the crisis of nationalism in India. This was not, however, a recommendation to stake the country's future upon a gamble, for the Mahatma was adamant in his belief that any politics confined to the predictable must be illusory. The fate of nations was determined, he thought, by forces that could neither be predicted nor claimed by anyone. And to press for a politics of responsibility in the face of this was only to suffer from delusions of grandeur. Thus Gandhi asked both Britain and the Muslim League to make a moral transformation possible by abandoning politics as the art of prediction and leaving India to God or anarchy. For as we have seen in earlier chapters, by invoking God the Mahatma was referring to something like the incalculable element in any history, one that he wished to prepare the ground for as one would to welcome a divine incarnation. The intensity of Gandhi's faith in this force was such that he spoke of its work following Britain's longed-for departure in the most passionate terms:

But it won't be the work of human hands. It will be the work of a Force—incalculable and invisible—which works, often upsetting all our calculations. I rely implicitly on it. Otherwise I should go mad in face of all this torrent of what I must call irritating criticism. They do not know my agony. I cannot express it except perhaps by dying.[10]

As it turns out Britain was not ready to depart her empire just yet, and though the Quit India Movement resulted in an uprising that at times degenerated into sabotage and terrorism, the colonial government jailed Gandhi and his associates only to free them for cordial negotiations after the war. The Muslim League, however, seems never to have recovered from the movement, which was seen as being the first of Gandhi's mobilizations to be directed against it as much as the government. And while the Mahatma tried vainly to come to an understanding with the League in the years that followed, whose high point arrived with the Gandhi-Jinnah talks of 1944, this method proved so unsuccessful that on the eve of the country's partition and independence he turned once again to the theme of God or anarchy. But this time, in the war's aftermath and with the British already preparing to leave, the political problem to be addressed had to do with the relations of Hindus and Muslims in the first instance, and of India and Pakistan in the second.

Yet by focussing so ferociously on the desultory negotiations between Congress and the League, as if they provided the only arena in which a new political relationship might be worked out for the two, historians have neglected Gandhi's repeated statements that a direct confrontation might be preferable to such pointless talks conducted through the mediation of the colonial government. Indeed the Mahatma had always maintained that honorable battle between equals was more likely to give rise to nonviolence than the chicanery of indirect negotiations. So referring to Hindu-Muslim violence in 1924, Gandhi remarked, "Fight I do not mind if it be fair, honourable, brave fighting between the two communities. But to-day it is all a story of unmitigated cowardice. They would throw stones and run away, murder and run away, go to court, put up false witnesses and cite false evidence. What a woeful record! How am I to make them brave?"[11] I shall explore the Mahatma's elaboration of this desire for civil war in the following section.

The hope of civil war

By the time he wrote to the Viceroy, Lord Mountbatten, on 8 May 1947, Gandhi knew that the British were soon about to leave India, but only after dividing it into two successor states. When asking Britain to give up her sense of political responsibility and leave without making such a settlement, however, the Mahatma no longer put forward the possibility of this departure forcing Congress and the League to resolve their differences in a popular government. Instead he told Mountbatten that if it had to come, such a partition should be decided by Indians themselves, for this was the only way they might be compelled to take responsibility for their future. The British should therefore concentrate on maintaining order until they left:

Whatever may be said to the contrary, it would be a blunder of the first magnitude for the British to be party in any way whatsoever to the division of India. If it has to come, let it come after the British withdrawal, as a result of understanding between the parties or of an armed conflict which according to Quaid-e-Azam Jinnah is taboo. [...] Whilst the British power is functioning in India, it must be held principally responsible for the preservation of peace in the country. That machine seems to be cracking under the existing strain which is caused by the raising of various hopes that cannot or must not be fulfilled.[12]

From the very beginning of his political career Gandhi had maintained that even if they did not wilfully encourage it in a policy of divide and rule, Britain's very presence in India polarized Hindus and Muslims by allowing them the luxury of refusing to deal directly with one another, such engagements as they had being conducted only through the mediation of the colonial state. For when they were not threatening a disturbance whose administrative consequences had to borne by this state, these parties were offering themselves up to be used by it against one another. And the Mahatma was clear that this situation was made possible by imperialism, which established the British as a neutral or third party between Indians, who themselves were rendered politically irresponsible by their lack of administrative power. Rather than worrying about the responsibility owed India by Britain, then, Gandhi thought that it was Indians who needed to cultivate such political responsibility, which they could do by dealing directly with one another. But this would only happen when they were left alone and tested through the suffering produced by their own violence. Thus Gandhi suggested that the Viceroy should disband the fractious interim government that had been set up between Britain, Congress and the League, and leave all power to a single party, which must therefore bear full responsibility for India's governance:

Meantime the Interim Government should be composed either of Congressmen or those whose names the Congress chooses or of Muslim League men or those whom the League chooses. The dual control of today, lacking team work and team spirit, is harmful for the country. The parties exhaust themselves in the effort to retain their seat and to placate you. [...] If you are not to leave a legacy of chaos behind, you have to make your choice and leave the Government of the whole of India [...] to one party.[13]

While none of the parties struggling over the future of India was likely to take him seriously, the Mahatma, who was dismissed by many of them as a woolly idealist, turned out in this the final phase of his career to be the most hard-headed of all these self-proclaimed realists. For the British, who wanted to fulfil what they saw as their political responsibility by minimizing the possibility of civil war in a partition of the country, or the Congress and League, who feared the loss of power, control and therefore independence in such a situation, were all driven by fear and the threat of violence. But Gandhi realized that atrocious as it was, the violent breakdown of administration that was occurring in different parts of the country could by no means be compared to a war of the kind that had just been concluded around the world. Indeed he was willing to risk even more violence, if only it would compel Indians to deal directly with each other. So in an interview to Reuter on 5 May 1947, he went so far as to say that it was perhaps the lack of an armed struggle against Britain that had prevented the development of a single nationality among Indians, but that this might yet be forged in civil war that brought Hindus and Muslims into direct and unmediated conflict with one another:

> I have often said before but it does not suffer in value through repetition because every time I repeat it, it gains force: the British will have to take the risk of leaving India to chaos or anarchy. This is so because there has been no home rule; the [rule] has been imposed on the people. And, when you voluntarily remove that rule there might be no rule in the initial stage. It might have come about if we had gained victory by the force of arms. The communal feuds you see here are, in my opinion, partly due to the presence of the British. If the British were not here, we would still go through the fire, no doubt, but that fire would purify us.[14]

The price of conducting a nonviolent movement against the British, then, was internecine violence among Indians, though Gandhi confessed many times during this period to his realization that the nonviolence adopted by the Congress in the past had been born of weakness not strength, that it was merely passive resistance and thus had no transformative effect. Indeed he held that passive resistance was merely the preparation for an armed struggle. And it was perhaps due to their consciousness of this cowardly and perverted exercise of nonviolence that so many Indians now turned with redoubled violence against their neighbors, since they had after all failed to engage the colonial state by force of arms. But though the British could be met with what Gandhi called the nonviolence of the weak, this was not possible in the far more intimate relations subsisting between Hindus and Muslims, where only the nonviolence of the strong was possible. In this way, therefore, even the most violent aspects of their relationship offered the possibility of a genuine nonviolence emerging, if only enough people were willing to sacrifice their lives in demonstrating its reality. The Mahatma frequently called for such sacrifices, and celebrated this nonviolence of the strong when he discovered instances of it, as for example in a mass meeting on 6 September 1947, in Calcutta, when he referred to the martyrdom of two such nonviolent warriors, saying that "such innocent deaths were necessary to keep the two communities together".[15]

It was evident to Gandhi that though millions of ordinary Indians were prepared for a civil war, and some among them even desired one, neither Congress nor the League, to say nothing of the British, were willing to countenance it. And so it was as much the refusal of these parties to heed his advice about the desirability of internecine warfare, as it was the much-noted neglect of Indians to behave non-violently, that made the Mahatma into a lonely and despondent figure in 1947. And yet he was by no means the only advocate of peace to prefer a civil war in India, as the retired civil servant Sir Malcolm Darling found on several occasions when travelling across the country on horseback in 1946–7. Meeting the Sardar of Kot, a wealthy Punjabi landowner whom he describes as a universally admired figure and a political independent, Darling noted in his diary the views of this Muslim, which appear identical to those being broadcast by Gandhi. The Sardar told Darling that the British should hand power over to the interim government conducted by the Congress and League as soon as possible and vacate India. If this didn't force the two parties into a settlement with one another, he said, then a civil war was preferable, since it would bring things to a head and transform the entire situation. But what, Darling retorted, of the peasants he had been meeting along his way who wanted the British to stay, as it was only from them that they expected *insaf* or justice? The Sardar's response was significant: *insaf*, he said, had lost its primary meaning of justice and now only meant security, serving therefore as a sign of fear rather than a precondition of freedom.[16]

The important point to recognize in these discussions of civil war is that for Gandhi and a number of his countrymen, promoting nonviolence did not contradict the toleration and even incitement of violence, since these were all intertwined in such a way that one was capable of offering an opening to the other. Thus the despair evident in his words of longing for anarchy at a prayer meeting in the year of independence:

> The Viceroy says that his task is merely to see that the British carry on their task honestly till power is transferred and then quit in peace. The British people do not wish that chaos should reign after they quit this country. I had already said that they should not worry about anarchy. I am, after all, a gambler. But who would listen to me? You do not listen to me. The Muslims have given me up. Nor can I fully convince the Congress of my point of view.[17]

Because he was unable to convince the Congress to hold out against partition to the bitter end, Gandhi reluctantly advised its members to accept the settlement that had been negotiated with Britain and the League, though he was against the very pragmatism of its terms, which had, after all, been dictated only under the threat of violence. "My view", he said to some visitors, "was that no one could take an inch of land by resorting to violence and murder. Let the whole country be reduced to ashes".[18] So at a meeting of the Congress called to confirm or reject its Working Committee's agreement with the Viceroy's project of partition, the Mahatma very politely accused the party's members of being complicit in the political division they claimed so much to dislike:

> So many things are happening today which bring to mind the English saying about swallowing a camel and straining at a gnat. The decision that has been arrived at has been reached with your complicity and yet you complain of the Working Committee, the Working Committee which has men of such great calibre on it. Those people had always said that the

Congress would not accept Pakistan and I was opposed to Pakistan even more. However we may leave aside my position. The decision has not been mine to take and the Working Committee has accepted it because there was no other way. They now see it clearly that the country is already divided into two camps. But our constitution permits it and your duty demands it that if you feel the Working Committee is in the wrong you should remove it, you should revolt and assume all power. You have a perfect right to do so, if you feel that you have the strength. But I do not find that strength in us today. If you had it I would also be with you and if I felt strong enough myself I would, alone, take up the flag of revolt. But today I do not see the conditions for doing so.[19]

Having resigned himself to India's partition, the Mahatma went on to suggest that it represented only the secret desire of the Congress, and that furthermore this division of the land would be amply justified if Hindus were to dominate over all others in the new India:

In the three-quarters of the country that has fallen to our share Hinduism is going to be tested. If you show the generosity of true Hinduism, you will pass in the eyes of the world. If not you will have proved Mr. Jinnah's thesis that Muslims and Hindus are two separate nations, that Hindus will forever be Hindus and Muslims forever Muslims, that the two will never unite, and that the Gods of the two are different. If, therefore, the Hindus present at this meeting claim that India is their country and in it Hindus will have a superior status, then it will mean that the Congress has not made a mistake and that the Working Committee has only done what you secretly wanted. [...] It does not matter if the land is divided. But if we divide the hearts then what the Congress Working Committee has done has been well done.[20]

Accepting the territorial division of the country, however, did not mean acquiescing in the division of hearts, and so Gandhi now dedicated his efforts not only to fostering what he called "heart unity" among the Hindus and Muslims of India, but also between the newly emerging states of India and Pakistan. With partition already decided, then, the Mahatma relinquished his talk of civil war but not the demand for a direct and unmediated relationship between Congress and the League that such a war might have made possible. So in a speech at one of his prayer meetings, Gandhi spoke again about his intuition that only without British or indeed any outside involvement could Indians and Pakistanis take responsibility for their own fate, and thus come to an understanding that might prevent their independence being blighted by continuing violence, which this time would occur between two sovereign states and their armies:

> Last evening I told you why it was that the prospect of freedom that is about to be ours did not fill me with joy. Today I wish to tell you how you can turn a bad thing into a good thing. What has happened has happened. Nothing is to be gained by brooding over it or blaming others. In legal terms it will be only a few days before freedom comes into effect. All the parties have arrived at an agreement and they cannot go back upon their word. Only God can undo what man has decided to do.
>
> The easiest way would be for the Congress and the League to come to an understanding without the intervention or the help of the Viceroy. In this the League would have to take the first step. I do not in the least imply by this that the decision about Pakistan should be undone. It should be taken as final, no more open to discussion now. But if ten representatives of either party sit together in a mud hut and resolve that they will not leave the hut till they have arrived at an understanding, then I can say that the decision they arrive at will be a thousand times better than the present Bill which is before the British Parliament and which envisages the setting up of two Dominions. If all the Hindus and Muslims who come to see me or write to me do not deceive me, then it is clear that no one is happy with the division of India. They all accept it against their will.[21]

But even this attempt to attain a genuine agreement and understanding about partition was to bear no fruit, and Gandhi was left struggling to quell disturbances in Bengal, Bihar and Delhi by the force of his example, while at the same time urging the normalization of relations between the two new states by gestures of reciprocity and goodwill. The story of these efforts, which led finally to Gandhi's assassination, is well known, and demonstrates his ability to rise above the fog of emotions like fear, betrayal and vengeance that prevented so many others from realizing the political implications of their actions. As it turns out, of course, the Mahatma's warnings about the violent future that awaited both India and Pakistan if they did not regularize their relations with each other proved all too prescient. But was it not precisely his "hard hearted" toleration of violence that allowed Gandhi to see past his compatriots and recommend a course of action that might establish a politics of nonviolence in both the successor states of Britain's Indian empire? Indeed it was noted by many who met him during this period that while the Mahatma was deeply anguished by the violence that accompanied partition, he remained for the most part not only unsentimental about it but even cheerful. At a speech during his prayer meeting on 4 November 1947, Gandhi described the effort that he made to remain emotionally detached from the horror of such circumstances, and in doing so to maintain a degree of balance and equipoise that exhibited a political realism far superior to that advocated by those who called for a solution involving more violence:

> These days practically all my time is spent in listening to the tales of woe from the Hindu or Sikh refugees or the Muslims of Delhi who are in distress. I also feel the same distress in my heart and am equally hurt. But I would not be truly non-violent if I started shedding tears or became gloomy. If non-violence made me so very soft, I would be crying the whole time, and there would be no time left to worship God, and to eat and sleep. But right from my childhood, being a follower of non-violence, I have made it a habit of hardening my heart instead of shedding tears while hearing or seeing any tragedy, so that I would be able to face them. Have not our saints and sages taught us that one who is a worshipper of ahimsa should be softer than a flower and harder than a stone?[22]

Just as he had always advised others to refuse the lure of exceptional circumstances that called for exceptional measures, so the Mahatma now put his words into practice by dealing with the situation that faced him in the most quotidian of ways. This he did in his dealings with the Hindu and Sikh refugees he met, many of whom were both the victims and perpetrators of violence, as well as in his daily routines that included friendships, jokes and laughter. For Gandhi realized that overpowering sentiments and the new kind of everyday reality they created were more likely to foster violence than the detachment he recommended. It is important to point out here that such emotions, especially when vicariously shared, are as much productive of humanitarian assistance and outrage as they are of that behaviour deemed intolerable and inhuman. And in this sense Gandhi, who appeared to recognize the profound relationship that existed between these opposites, was certainly not a proponent of such sentiments. In fact apart from departing the conventions of pacifist ethics by recommending the violence of a civil war, he repeatedly urged people to tolerate and even minimize their sufferings in order to make possible the moral transformation of their enemies, thus treating them not as victims to be administered to by humanitarian assistance but moral agents whose actions were crucial in defining not only their own future but also that of their tormentors. But this could only happen, he thought, by refusing the help of any third party, a figure he distrusted in all its incarnations, from the colonial state to a national one and, as we shall see shortly, an international body like the United Nations as well.

A violent unity

With the partition of India an accomplished fact, the direct dealing Gandhi longed to see between Hindus and Muslims became an even more improbable occurrence. For not only did the discussions between Congress and the League now have to take the form of international relations, but a civil war, too, had become impossible as another way of establishing such dealings. And the violence that remained between Hindus, Sikhs and Muslims in both countries was, as the Mahatma realized, nothing but a degrading attack on minority populations, possessing no potential for a true contest between equals that might decide the fate of either nation. Indeed this violence was proving so intractable precisely because it did not constitute any kind of direct dealing between the communities, but referred instead to deeds that were happening in another country. For if members of all three communities were killing each other in one country for the violence their coreligionists had suffered in the other, the refugees fleeing in both directions were doing nothing but wreaking vengeance upon those whom they saw as the partners of their tormentors in the country left behind. Such violence, in other words, was as indirect as it was possible to be, because its rage was directed not at the victims at hand so much as those who were now unreachable in another country.

And yet this violence was not simply abstract in its hatred of all the Hindus, Muslims or Sikhs attacked, since if anything it demonstrated the inability of these groups to separate one from the other, as the separation of India and Pakistan should have prompted them to do. If anything the constant reference to what was happening in the other country only proved in some perverse way the Mahatma's contention that India and Pakistan were not separate nations but entwined in the most intimate fashion, though their relationship could now only be revealed in the form of mutual devastation. But this of course made it impossible to deal with violence in one country without reference to the other, and so Gandhi's attempts to foster nonviolence had to operate in both, by building upon the link of death and destruction that held India and Pakistan together in order to transform their relationship. For it was only when these countries were treated as a single unit that the murderous relations between Muslims on the one side and Hindus and Sikhs on the other might be seen as equivalent, and indeed as representing the paradoxical efforts of each community to claim moral agency for itself rather than merely assuming the status of victims. And it was to this agency that the Mahatma had to appeal in order to push the cause of nonviolence, asking members of all religious groups to act in such a way as to transform the behaviour of their enemies across the border.

Once partition had been conceded, and even before its riots and the refugees they created had begun, Gandhi tried hard to maintain links between the two countries, realizing that only these would be capable of withstanding the coming wave of violence. Initially the Mahatma tried to forge such links by objecting to the division of the army into two hostile forces that he knew would be used against each other, then by rejecting the division of the provinces of Bengal and Punjab in terms of their religious geography, as this would deprive India and Pakistan of a shared population and therefore alienate them even further from one another. Jinnah, of course, had also resisted the partition of these provinces, and was perhaps unfairly interpreted as doing so in order to gain more territory for Pakistan, while retaining the large Hindu and Sikh minorities in it as "hostages" to guarantee India's good behaviour towards her Muslim minority. But just as the division had been forced upon Jinnah by the same argument he used for the partition of colonial India, so too did the Mahatma reject sectioning the provinces on the same grounds that he refused to countenance the country's division, saying that one kind of partition did not justify another. And while this could have meant handing Punjab and Bengal to Pakistan in their entirety, it would also have resulted in that country being deprived of an absolute Muslim majority, which might well have been Jinnah's desire as well.

Like the Mahatma, then, his Pakistani rival spent much of the year that was left to him after independence urging Hindus and Sikhs not to leave the country, and even accusing India of trying to shut Pakistan down by drawing out these large minority populations together with their capital and skills.[23] Apart from recognizing their value to his new country, Jinnah's attitude to these minority populations also had a principle behind it, since his struggle to divide India had been fought not in order to make Muslims an absolute majority in their own country, just as Hindus were in India, but rather to break up these communities so as to allow for a democratic politics in both countries that was no longer based on religion.[24] Whatever the merits were of Jinnah's principles, his actions did overlap in some respects with those of the Mahatma's, though both failed to stem the flow of refugees. And faced with failure on all fronts, Gandhi now concentrated on making sure that India fulfilled her contractual agreements to Pakistan as far as the transfer to her of funds and goods promised under the partition agreement was concerned. Far more important, however, were his efforts to make possible the return of refugees from both countries and the restitution of their properties. So in speeches made at his prayer meetings the Mahatma made it clear that only actions dedicated to a change of hearts across the border would be able resolve the violence within each country:

If all the Muslims go away to Pakistan and all the Hindus and Sikhs come to India, then we would become permanent enemies. And then we would be fighting to our hearts' content. Let us save ourselves from such an absurd situation.[25]

I know that if there is a change of heart in one place the same thing will happen at other places. If we have a change of heart here there will be a change of heart in Pakistan. It will take some effort no doubt but there will be a change. After all madness seized us only after it had seized people in Pakistan. I shall not go into the various stages and degrees of madness. If sanity does not return we shall lose both India and Pakistan. There will be a war. The present state cannot last. People say that the required change in the situation has already taken place, that Hindus and Sikhs have come to India and Muslims from India have gone to Pakistan. They point out that transfer of populations of such magnitude cannot be reversed. I do not hold this view. Even if I am the only one to say it I shall still say that so long as people do not go back to their homes there will be no peace in the two countries. All the comforts you can provide to the Sikh and Hindu refugees are not going to heal the wounds they have suffered. It will be a matter of perpetual distress to them that they have lost their hearths and homes and if there is a war in fifty years' time or a hundred years' time, they are going to remember this. Such things are not forgotten.[26]

Such statements were by no means exercises in self-delusion, as news from across the border did have great impact on the actions of those who lived in both Pakistan and India, thus giving the lie to historical accounts that would explain the events following partition either as the product of fear and hatred or simply the result of efforts at securing some material advantage in disturbed circumstances. Despite his quickly eroding power in India, for example, the Mahatma's pronouncements were followed closely by Pakistanis, and the great fast he undertook to stop anti-Muslim violence in Delhi not only brought him entreaties and promises from many in Pakistan, but also played a part in calming the frenzy there as it did in India. Indeed even at the height of animosity between Hindus and Muslims, both before and after independence, Gandhi continued receiving a stream of visitors and correspondence from members of the Muslim League. These interlocutors were often hostile, challenging the Mahatma to prove his claims that he was a friend of the Muslims, but even so they indicated a barely-concealed desire to believe in him. Many of these communications were, after all, appeals to Gandhi, asking him to prove his friendship by doing something for Muslims.

Of these appeals perhaps the most important were from Muslim Leaguers who asked the Mahatma to show his concern for their co-religionists by going to Bihar following the large-scale killings of Muslims in that province in 1946. These riots were themselves fomented as retaliation for the killing of Hindus in Bengal, which had taken Gandhi to the affected district of Noakhali in an effort to create a change of heart and allow for the return of refugees there. And when the Mahatma went to

Bihar, which he did after the violence in Bengal had sufficiently abated, he was accused by his Hindu opponents of betraying them for Muslims and asked to return and prove himself all over again. This curious mixture of hostility and affection was displayed by his enemies throughout Gandhi's career, its last manifestation prompted by his promise to walk to Pakistan, as if in a final performance of celebrated processions like the Salt March or his solitary walk through Noakhali. By going to Pakistan, from where he had already received invitations and assurances of support, the Mahatma wanted to claim both countries as his own, and work for the cause of Hindus and Sikhs oppressed there as he had for Muslims in India. But Gandhi realized that his mission to Pakistan could only succeed if peace returned to Delhi first, responding to the taunt that he should leave India by saying that "Hindu and Sikh refugees and others here have to prove by being friendly with the Muslims here that I need not stay on in Delhi any longer. Then I would rush to Pakistan with full confidence that my going there would not be in vain".[27] Before he could embark on his march Gandhi was assassinated by a man who, like so many of his enemies, claimed to love and hate him at the same time, shooting the Mahatma to prevent his final betrayal by Muslims.

The part-challenge and part-desire in the approach of so many among Gandhi's bitterest enemies, Hindu and Muslim nationalists included, not only illustrates the remarkable persuasiveness of his politics, but also tells us how difficult it was for the Mahatma's foes to decide whether he was transparent in his sincerity or, on the contrary, a consummate hypocrite. In other words while his friends might well have accused Gandhi of being mistaken about some decision or other, or even of being quite irrational at times, extraordinary about the accusations of his enemies has always been their almost obsessive focus on the possibility that he was insincere. And among them were not only Gandhi's Indian rivals but also Winston Churchill, who thought him to be "the world's most successful humbug" and as prime minister devoted precious time during the war wondering, in letters to the viceroy, if he was doing things like secretly adding glucose into his few ounces of orange juice taken during a fast in order to keep going.[28] Not so much the ill effects of the Mahatma's politics, then, but his potential for hypocrisy proved to be the dividing line between those who supported and opposed him, for even considering Gandhi to have been deluded would show enough faith in his principles to put one in the former group and not the latter. Consumed by suspicion and determined to prove the Mahatma's insincerity by analyzing his words and actions much more carefully than they would those of any other leader, his enemies were compelled in this way to take Gandhi's morality more seriously than his friends, who could after all satisfy themselves with what they approved of in his politics for the basest of motives. Gandhi's failure, in other words, was in some measure also his success, rendering the truth or falsity of his intentions irrelevant.

The ocean on fire

While the Mahatma's fasts and finally his assassination had an undeniable effect in stilling the fury of partition violence, both in India and Pakistan, its scale was so unprecedented that he sometimes despaired of finding a way to counter it. Gandhi frequently used a phrase during this period to describe the difficulties facing him, saying that when the ocean itself was on fire no resort could be found to quench the flames. At times this lack of a source for nonviolence made the Mahatma advise concerned friends to go about their lives and stop worrying about a situation they couldn't alter. But he also began to conceive of the possibility that the ocean of fire might itself provide the resources of nonviolence. Instead of fighting fire with fire, however, Gandhi recommended that the war brewing between India and Pakistan over the disputed princely state of Kashmir could, in compelling direct dealings between the two countries, produce nonviolence as its outcome. Though it would be a conflict very different from the civil war he had once hoped for, Gandhi thought that such a war might provide an opening for peace in both countries, but not one based on the victory of either. What did his tacit support of this war imply, and how did the Mahatma justify it given his advice to Britain on dealing even with the Nazis in a nonviolent way?

To begin with it is important to note that such a struggle had almost been set up to occur by Britain's refusal to transfer its so-called paramountcy over the autonomous territories of many hundreds of princely states to the new governments of India and Pakistan. Gandhi had indeed pleaded for these feudatories propped up by British rule to be integrated into the empire's successor states, realizing that their theoretical freedom either to remain independent or accede to one of the new dominions would push the latter into a dangerous competition for the support of as many princes as possible so as to augment their territorial advantages. Just as they had insisted upon dividing India as part of their political responsibility to her various peoples, however, the British also refused on the same principle to hand paramountcy over the princely states to their successors. Speculation has never ceased on why a departing colonial power should want to leave behind these principalities as cockpits of future strife, though it might be in keeping with the principles by which Gandhi worked to see in both these acts the performance of a moral duty as much as anything else.

The Mahatma's forebodings were justified when the two largest of Britain's native states held off acceding to either country once independence was achieved. On the one hand the Muslim ruler of Hyderabad, with its majority Hindu population, tried to preserve his autonomy while helping Pakistan address its financial difficulties with a large loan; and on the other the Hindu ruler of Kashmir, with its predominantly Muslim population, occupied himself with a similar balancing act while trying to pacify a movement for democracy in the state led by Sheikh Abdullah. And so when armed tribesmen from Pakistan who may or may not have been supported by that country's government crossed into Kashmir and made their way to its capital, the Maharaja acceded to India and Nehru flew troops into the principality to repel this invasion. Thus began the first India-Pakistan war, resulting in a resort to the United Nations and the state's division between the two countries, whose border remains disputed by both and unrecognized in international law to this day. While deprecating war and calling for a peaceful resolution to the conflict, Gandhi ended up supporting the deployment of Indian troops to Kashmir, though he did so with the bitter recognition that following their independence, the successor states of Britain's empire were now logically committed to a politics that included war among its means. So in a speech at his prayer meeting on 26 September 1947, the Mahatma had the following to say:

> Let us arrive at a mutual and friendly settlement. Why can we not do so? We Hindus and Muslims were friends till yesterday. Have we become such enemies today that we cannot trust one another? If you say that you are never going to trust them, then the two sides would have to fight. Speaking in terms of logic it may be asked what else would people do when they have army and police and are forced to depend upon them? [...] We should not take the offensive. But we must be ready to fight, because when war comes it does not come after giving a warning. We should not take any initiative to fight, but if the other side takes the initiative, both the Governments face their doom. War is no joke. After all, how long can I go on stressing the point? But if there is no settlement between the two sides, there would be no alternative. In that event, if all the Hindus have to die fighting, I would not be sorry. But we have to choose the path of justice. I would not bother if all the Hindus and all the Muslims have to die following that path.[29]

Was this a counsel of despair, or had Gandhi finally come to admit the necessity of war, and even to justify its morality? We know that during this period, when he seemed suddenly to have lost the ability to mobilize a following, the Mahatma rejected the congratulations that were offered him for India's independence, considering himself a moral bankrupt. It was not enough that he and a few others should recognize the truth of nonviolence while the rest did not, for Gandhi had often said that he wanted to die a successful man and not simply be reduced into a prophet of the future. The intensely practical cast of his mind meant that the Mahatma continued searching for an opportunity to manifest the virtues of nonviolence, and the devastation of partition together with the war over Kashmir posed, therefore, the greatest challenge he had faced. It is Gandhi's response to this challenge that I want to describe here, by looking at how he sought to turn the conflict in Kashmir into an opportunity for nonviolence, while at the same time admitting neither to war's morality nor indeed its necessity.

During his prayer meeting of 5 November 1947, Gandhi referred to a letter he had received asking how he could support a war over Kashmir. Saying that it was a question "worth asking and also not worth asking",[30] the Mahatma went on to quote the letter:

The question is: "You advised even the British to follow the path of nonviolence when they were facing defeat. You advised them to give up arms and become non-violent. You could show that much courage there; then why don't you ask the Government of the country to fight a non-violent battle?"[31]

Why was such a question not worth asking? Because, suggested the Mahatma, he was no longer in a position to advise anybody, not least because he was unable to influence the government:

I have already stated that I am a nobody and no one listens to me. People say that the Sardar is my man and Panditji is also but mine and Maulana too is my man. They are all mine and also not mine. I have never abandoned my non-violence. I have been training myself in non-violence and it was acceptable till we attained independence. Now they wonder how they can rule with non-violence. And then there is the army and they have taken the help of the army. Now I am of no value at all.[32]

From a question that was both worth asking and not, to politicians who were his men and who were not, Gandhi's equivocal words were a commentary on the seduction of power. They also hinted that the government's lack of courage in transforming the nature of politics in a truly revolutionary way was due to its adoption of the old British ethic of responsibility, something that Congress had itself fought against not so long ago. In these circumstances he could only look to the possibilities opened up for nonviolence at the very limits of "responsible" government, in a war where courage and sacrifice inevitably exceeded the calculations of political interest by their far more profound existential depths:

Hence, I still stand by what I had conveyed to Hitler, Mussolini, Churchill and the people of Japan. I say the same thing to our Government. But in Kashmir Sheikh Abdullah is giving a brave fight—I have always admired bravery. It is true that he believes in violence but it requires courage and I do admire it. I admire even Subhas Babu not because I approved of his violence but because I could never have formed the Azad Hind Fauj. When I see something good and fail to give it due credit, I cannot be truly non-violent. I have no doubt that if Sheikh Abdullah fights it to the last and keeps the Hindus and Sikhs with him, it is bound to have a great impact on the people here. However, if I could have my way of non-violence and everybody listened to me, we would not send our army as we are doing now. And if we did send, it would be a non-violent army. It would be a non-violent fight if our people went there and gladly met their death at the hands of the Afridis. It would be a non-violent war because they would be dying remaining non-violent.[33]

Having praised not only Sheikh Abdullah but also an old enemy, Subhas Chandra Bose and his army of German and Japanese-sponsored turncoats, Gandhi went on to repeat that he was no longer in any position to recommend nonviolent resistance, and so could only discover virtue in the existential aspects of daring and suffering that were brought to light in extreme forms of violence. In any case the armed resistance in Kashmir, because it brought together Hindus, Muslims and Sikhs and constituted a real struggle, not simply a degrading killing of minorities, had much to commend it in comparison to the partition riots:

> In his time Mr. Churchill could not say, but today, Sheikh Abdullah and the army which has gone there can tell me that my non-violence has failed in Delhi where acts of barbarism are being committed and what they are doing is not barbaric. And I must admit that they have a right to say that. But they cannot tell me anything if I can convince all the Hindus, Muslims and the Sikhs of the Union about my non-violence. In that event, I could myself go with a non-violent army to Kashmir or Pakistan or any place, and then my work would become very easy. And then, the impact of non-violence would be so great that it would be worth seeing. [...] The delegates from Britain, China, the U.S.A. and Pakistan who came to attend the Asian Regional Conference praised me for my work. But their praise hurts me. Today I have become bankrupt. I have no say with my people today. What I said in the past has no value. I will be worthy of praise only when I can influence people. But that is not the situation today. I am merely expressing my helplessness before you.[34]

The fact that he lent the war such equivocal support, however, didn't mean that the Mahatma saw it as being nothing more than an imperfect instrument to achieve his goals, for this would have contradicted his most deeply held principles. Indeed it was precisely because he was unable to control the war that Gandhi could support it, since only in this way would it cease to be a means to some end. His ambivalent support for the war, therefore, was dictated at least in theory by the hope that it might offer an opportunity for nonviolence, something the Mahatma was duty bound to encourage. In time Gandhi came to place much more weight on what he saw as an exemplary battle in

LEAVING INDIA TO ANARCHY

Kashmir, one that united the state's Muslim majority with its Hindu and Sikh minorities against the Afridi invaders from across the border. It was a battle, moreover, revealing the existence of that virtue which the Mahatma prized most, fratricide in the way of righteousness. And this time it was the fratricide of Muslims, the very thing that Pakistani propaganda condemned as the worst of sins, which had come to illustrate the teaching of the *Bhagavad-Gita*:

The poison which has spread among us should never have spread. Through Kashmir that poison might be removed from us. If they make such a sacrifice in Kashmir to remove that poison, then our eyes also would be opened.[35]

Today Hinduism and Islam are being tested on the soil of Kashmir. If the right thing is done and the right direction given to the process the chief actors will win fame. It is my prayer that in the present darkness in the country Kashmir may become the star that provides light.[36]

Kashmir might well do wonders in restoring communal peace in India, but what about her relations with Pakistan? Gandhi had hoped that the conflict would force India and Pakistan finally to deal directly with each other, which is to say honestly and without bluster, but much to his chagrin they turned to the United Nations instead. And by doing so the Mahatma thought they had introduced a third party into their relationship, something that would only encourage Pakistan and India to posture even more, this time by drawing upon the support of others on the international stage. In decrying the necessity of arbitration, of course, Gandhi was being true to the oldest of his principles, which entailed the rejection of any mediation, like that offered by lawyers to their clients or even doctors to their patients, as entailing a loss of moral sovereignty and the consequent strengthening of the hold that illness or litigation had upon one.[37] Now mediation, of course, is not something that can be eliminated from human relations, and so we might well see Gandhi's obsession with direct dealing as being unrealistic. But then he was concerned with mediators and third parties only in certain contexts and not others. At issue in law, medicine or indeed politics, was the fact that men and women were being manipulated and sacrificed in the service of future ends, thus reducing their social relations to nothing but a calculus of violence.

Peculiar though his views on doctors and lawyers may seem in retrospect, it was clear to the Mahatma that whatever their benefits, these colonial professions were responsible for maintaining British rule in India, if only by controlling the relations that people had with each other as much as with their own bodies through a set of state-regulated institutions. International mediation was no better, since by lending one or both rivals outside support it risked entrenching their conflict, even if only in some kind of tolerable stasis governed by a cease-fire agreement as the dispute over Kashmir has been for well over half a century now. Not convinced that India's resort to the UN was the only way in which to prevent the escalation of violence with Pakistan, Gandhi worried that it would simply result in outsiders having more say in the politics of the region than Indians and Pakistanis themselves:

Mistakes were made on both sides. Of this I have no doubt. But this does not mean that we should persist in those mistakes, for then in the end we should only destroy ourselves in a war and the whole of the sub-continent will pass into the hands of some third power. That will be the worst imaginable fate for us. I shudder to think of it. Therefore the two Dominions should come together with God witness and find a settlement. The matter is now before the U.N.O. It cannot be withdrawn from there. But if India and Pakistan come to a settlement the big powers in the U.N.O. will have to endorse that settlement. They will not object to the settlement. They themselves can only say that they will do their best to see that the two countries arrive at an understanding through mutual discussions. Let us pray to God that He may spare us the threatened strife, but not at any price. All that we may pray to God is to grant that we may either learn to live in amity with each other or if we must fight to let us fight to the very end. That may be folly, but sooner or later it will purify us.[38]

LEAVING INDIA TO ANARCHY

In his rejection of third parties and advocacy of violent purification over an immoral peace, Gandhi was echoing in his discussion of partition the great themes of his politics from the Quit India Movement; and who is to say if his criticism of international mediation and cease-fires did not in the end prove correct? For in refusing to deal directly with one another, India and Pakistan have repeatedly had to rely upon external powers, and by doing so draw them into the region in a way that has made much of it into a battlefield for proxy wars to this day. Together with exaggerated notions of political responsibility and humanitarian intervention, in other words, the Mahatma realized that international peacekeeping more often than not sustained conflict rather than resolving it. And to this he preferred the purification of a war that offered far more in the way of opportunities for nonviolence. Such an attitude seems perverse only because it has become fashionable to treat life as an absolute value, which Gandhi did not, seeing in a duty to truth the only virtue that mattered. The Mahatma offers us the curious spectacle of a man who was prepared to recommend war though he had worked all his life for nonviolence. Yet Gandhi supported war not merely as a last option, nor even as an unavoidable deterrent, to say nothing of a punishment, but because he thought it held out more hope for nonviolence that anything the UN could propose.

Whether or not such a war waged out of love for one's enemy is possible, it is clear that the rivalry between India and Pakistan has always possessed an element of thwarted friendship about it. Even in colonial times, after all, the Muslim League's claims for parity with Congress, and finally Pakistan's separation from India, had been premised upon the idea that only some measure of political equality between Hindus and Muslims could make for a friendship between them.[39] After independence Pakistan has in many ways continued this quest for parity by means both fair and foul, trying to equalize her disparities of size, population and power compared to India by weakening the latter through terrorism, matching up to it by an arms race gone nuclear, or even by hoping that her neighbor might be fragmented into units of a more manageable size. And though Pakistan has only managed to partition herself in the process, the final aim of this long-lived desire is apparently nothing but the possibility of friendship without fear. This desire is evident during the wars fought between India and Pakistan, which have always been of the most rule-bound and textbook kind, fought outside civilian areas for the most part and replete with instances of old-fashioned chivalry and honor between the contending armies. And in this way they have differed from modern wars more generally, as also from the unmeasured violence of so much conflict within each of these countries. As Gandhi suggested so often, then, it has perhaps been in their wars alone that Pakistan and India have approached the direct dealings necessary for friendship between them.

CONCLUSION

Early in July of 1937, a well-known Nazi journalist, SS officer and advisor to Hitler named Roland von Strunk visited Gandhi at his ashram in Segaon. As befitted a National Socialist concerned with the cultivation of a nation's health and power, Captain Strunk was interested in the Mahatma's criticism of machinery and modern medicine. In the course of their conversation, Gandhi pointed out what he thought was the fundamental contradiction in the attention that Europeans paid to the preservation of life:

> But the West attaches an exaggerated importance to prolonging man's earthly existence. Until the man's last moment on earth you go on drugging him even by injecting. That, I think, is inconsistent with the recklessness with which they will shed their lives in war. Though I am opposed to war, there is no doubt that war induces reckless courage. Well, without ever having to engage in a war I want to learn from you the art of throwing away my life for a noble cause. But I do not want that excessive desire of living that Western medicine seems to encourage in man even at the cost of tenderness for subhuman life.[1]

Having expressed his horror of the hatreds sweeping Europe, the violence of Spain's civil war, in which he had participated on the side of Franco, and even what he said was the "overdone" targeting of Jews in Germany, Strunk must have been surprised to hear that Gandhi was in some ways even more contemptuous of life than Hitler. For the Mahatma's desire to learn from the "reckless courage" of European warfare was not in the least premised upon the need to protect one's own life, nor indeed the lives of one's countrymen, racial brothers or partners in civilization, as was true both of the Nazis and their enemies. In fact Gandhi was clear that justifying war by means of the conventional link between taking life in order to save it could in no sense be considered rational. What the Mahatma found disturbing, in other words, was not that an inordinate concern with preserving life stood opposed to its casual disposal in battle, but rather that one led to the other in such a way as to make the love of life itself guilty of the desire for death. Only by giving up the thirst for life that was represented in modern war and medicine alike, he suggested, could the urge to kill be tamed.

From the kind of "subhuman life" that modern medicine sacrificed in its vivisections, to men and women rendered "subhuman" and thus available for fascism's killing machines, Gandhi blamed humanity, or at least its definition in terms of life as an absolute value, for the massive scale of modern violence. And this not only allowed him to put the Nazis in the same category as their enemies as far as the espousal of such a value was concerned, but also to hold humanitarians and pacifists equally responsible for its violence. Indeed in some ways those dedicated to the cause of peace and humanity were even more culpable than the rest, if only because they might value life in far greater measure than others who were at least willing to sacrifice it in war. For in the very recklessness of this sacrifice the Mahatma saw the possibility of going beyond and even destroying life as an absolute value. The kind of violence that entailed risking one's life, in other words, was capable of providing an opening for nonviolence, something that preventing war in the name of life's sanctity never could. And this was why Gandhi wanted to learn the art of throwing one's life away from those features of European warfare that still involved such risk. As if convinced by the Mahatma's words, Roland von Strunk died in Germany a few

CONCLUSION

months later, the casualty of an old-fashioned duel fought with pistols, which resulted in Hitler banning the custom altogether.

It was only by refusing to treat life as an absolute value that Gandhi was able to accomplish his aim and spiritualize politics, for he thought that as long as life remained its basis political action could never answer to moral principles.[2] After all the preservation of life was an aim that all political actors shared, and therefore no moral principles could be drawn from it, these having been reduced merely to second-order justifications for valuing some lives over others. The courage of a Nazi, for instance, would be deemed in this way to possess less value than that displayed by an American or Russian soldier fighting him, but only because it was dedicated to taking life for an immoral cause. The paradoxical thing about the Mahatma's glorification of sacrifice in the name of an ideal rather than a gross reality such as life, however, is that its rejection of this reality as an absolute value also entailed protecting it. Only by disdaining life could it be saved, while even politics in its most sacrificial forms, including the Cold War doctrine of Mutually Assured Destruction, continued being devoted to life's preservation.

Gandhi went further than asking people not to love life, if only because he wanted them to love death more. Thus in his response to a letter from Bengal describing the exodus of Hindus from what had in 1947 become East Pakistan, he claimed that by loving death those in peril could avoid the cowardice that might save their lives but leave them consumed by shame and the consequent hatred of Muslims that was meant to atone for it:

Man does not live but to escape death. If he does so, he is advised not to do so. He is advised to learn to love death as well as life, if not more so. A hard saying, harder to act up to, one may say. Every worthy act is difficult. Ascent is always difficult. Descent is easy and often slippery. Life becomes liveable only to the extent that death is treated as a friend, never as an enemy. To conquer life's temptations, summon death to your aid. In order to postpone death a coward surrenders honor, wife, daughter and all. A courageous man prefers death to the surrender of self-respect.[3]

A life devoted solely to self-preservation, in other words, would not be one worth living. Though he was willing to tolerate spectacles of sacrificial destruction, Gandhi did not pay as much attention to such events in places like Stalingrad, Dresden or Hiroshima as did the politicians who waged war in the name of life. Instead his disregard for life in the name of principles took far more quotidian forms. So during the time he spent in Noakhali just prior to India's partition, trying to make possible the return of Hindu refugees there, the Mahatma repeatedly forbade private persons and charitable organizations to render them help. This was in order to compel the Muslim League government of Bengal to fulfill its responsibilities in caring for this displaced and terrorized population, while at the same time teaching the latter to behave as the citizens of a democracy. Nirmal Kumar Bose, in his luminous account of Gandhi's days in Calcutta and Noakhali during this period, makes it abundantly clear that the Mahatma's concerns were not in fact humanitarian at all but political, since it was in politics that the root of violence as well as its potential for conversion were lodged:

But, in spite of the magnitude of material damage, Gandhiji was more concerned about the political implications of the riots. Later on, he told me one day that he knew, in any war brutalities were bound to take place: war was a brutal thing. He was therefore not so much concerned about the actual casualties or the extent of material damage, but in discovering the political intentions working behind the move and the way of combating them successfully.[4]

The conversation with some friends who had come on behalf of the Gita Press of Gorakhpur had more than a usual interest. They came with an offer of blankets worth a lac of rupees for distribution among the evacuees. But Gandhiji wished them to hold back the gift for the present. He said, it was the duty of the Government to provide warm covering, and it was within the rights of the evacuees to press their demand. If the Government failed, and confessed that it had not resources enough, then only could private organizations step in to help the evacuees. Unless the people were conscious of their political rights and knew how to act in a crisis, democracy can never be built up.[5]

Gandhiji dealt with the problem as a whole and explained that we should proceed in such a manner that the Government might be put in the wrong and the struggle lifted to the necessary political plane. Whatever steps had to be taken, whether it was relief or migration, should be taken only after the Government had been made to confess that they were unable to do anything more for the sufferers, or had failed to restrain the rowdy Muslim elements. If, in the meantime, which he hoped would not be more than a week or so, a few of the sufferers died of exposure, he was hard-hearted enough (*main nirday hun*) not to be deflected from his course by such events. The whole struggle had to be lifted to the political plane; mere humanitarian relief was not enough, for it would fail to touch the root of the problem.[6]

My purpose in quoting Bose's text so extensively is not only to show that Gandhi's politics of nonviolence was as far removed from humanitarianism and its cult of victims as it could possibly be, but also to demonstrate how it was that his idealism was the least "idealistic" of things. So his response to suffering was not in the first instance to ameliorate it, but instead to make sure that those who had been wronged behaved like moral agents and not victims, thus allowing them to enter into a political relationship with their persecutors. These men, after all, were themselves in need of a moral transformation, for which their victims were to be made responsible, preferably without the humanitarian intervention of any third party. If the spiritualization of politics meant anything, it was this eminently realistic dedication to an ideal that took precedence over life's own reality. And in fact the nihilistic or even apocalyptic elements in modern politics all seem to derive from the fears of those who value life either in its weightiest forms, as represented by the survival of nations, races and even species, or in its lightest and most impoverished ones, such as the desire to safeguard one's profit, lifestyle or wellbeing, both forms being part of the same continuum. For it is the fear of this value being threatened that makes possible a defensive politics with no limits as far as its violence is concerned.

When in 1947 he was asked to express his opinion on what might go into a report for the United Nations Human Rights Commission in Geneva, which was to draft the Universal Declaration of Human Rights, Gandhi rejected the whole idea of inalienable rights. Chief among these, of course, was the right to life, which like all other rights the Mahatma would make dependent on duties instead, since these had nothing passive about them and involved dealing with violence in an effort to convert it.[7] Indeed it was precisely in violence that Gandhi claimed to discover the possibility of its overcoming, something that the great revolutionary figures of the past two centuries had always maintained, though none in his intensely moral if also idiosyncratic way. It was the moral relationship between enemies rather than friends that created rights, which meant that such relationships had to be prized despite the violence they entailed, and not what the Mahatma considered the deeply suspect ideal of life as an absolute value. It might be appropriate, then, to end this book with a passage from Gandhi's letter to Julian Huxley, the first Director of UNESCO, condemning the rights of man:

> I learnt from my illiterate but wise mother that all rights to be deserved and preserved came from duty well done. Thus the very right to live accrues to us only when we do the duty of citizenship of the world. From this one fundamental statement, perhaps it is easy enough to define the duties of man and woman and correlate every right to some corresponding duty to be first performed. Every other right can be shown to be usurpation hardly worth fighting for. I wonder if it is too late to revise the idea of defining the rights of man apart from his duty.[8]

If Gandhi's vision of nonviolence is to be taken at all seriously today, we ought to acknowledge that one of the great challenges facing its proponents is to think about what a "citizenship of the

CONCLUSION

world" might look like that does not invoke the rights of man as its justification. For unlike rights, which can only be guaranteed by states and are thus never truly in the possession of those who bear them, duties belong to individuals and cannot be stripped from them.[9] They represent in this sense the inalienable sovereignty of men and women, and therefore stand alone in their ability to create rights. Yet first among all duties, of course, is the disposal rather than preservation of life, something that is familiar enough from our own notions of morality and politics, or at least such of them as stand outside the demesne of rights. Indeed it is even possible to say that duty is dominated by death and the individual, as right is by life and the collective. By thinking of duties before rights, then, Gandhi was able to think of sovereignty beyond the state and its violent politics of life. Nothing, surely, could be more revolutionary than such a task, which remains to be accomplished in a time marked by the fragmentation of sovereignty itself in the global arena.

NOTES

INTRODUCTION

1. Kanji Dwarkadas, *India's Fight for Freedom, 1913–1937: An Eyewitness Story* (Bombay: Popular Prakashan, 1966), p. 458.
2. Kanji Dwarkadas, *Gandhiji Through My Diary Leaves, 1915–1948* (Bombay: Vakil and Sons, 1950), p. 22.
3. Nirmal Kumar Bose, *My Days With Gandhi* (New Delhi: Orient Longman, 1999), p. 106.
4. M. K. Gandhi, "Hindu University Speech", in *Speeches and Writings of Mahatma Gandhi* (Madras: G. A. Natesan and Co., 1922), p. 256.
5. See M. K. Gandhi, *Hind Swaraj and Other Writings*, ed. Anthony J. Parel (Cambridge: Cambridge University Press, 1997), p. 73.

1. BASTARD HISTORY

1. The only exception, who thus proves the rule, is the Jain philosopher Raychandra, known as Raychandbhai, for who see M. K. Gandhi, *An Autobiography or The Story of my Experiments with Truth*, trans. Mahadev Desai (Ahmedabad: Navajivan Trust, 2009), pp. 73–75.
2. See V. D. Savarkar, *The Indian War of Independence* (Bombay: Hind, 1946).
3. See John William Kaye and George Bruce Malleson, *Kaye's and Malleson's History of the Indian Mutiny of 1857-8* (London: W. H. Lane, 1888–9).
4. See, for instance, Karl Marx, "The revolt in the Indian army", *New York Daily Tribune*, 15 July 1857, "The revolt in India", *New York Daily Tribune*, 4 August 1857, "The Indian question", *New York Daily Tribune*, 14 August 1857, and "The Indian revolt", *New York Daily*

Tribune, 16 September 1857, in Karl Marx and Friedrich Engels, *On Colonialism* (Moscow: Progress Publishers, 1983), pp. 130–33, 134–37, 138–42, 152–55.
5. See for this Christopher Herbert, *War of no Pity: The Indian Mutiny and Victorian Trauma* (Princeton: Princeton University Press, 2008).
6. For this argument see Hannah Arendt, "Imperialism", in *The Origins of Totalitarianism* (San Diego: Harcourt Brace and Co., 1979), pp. 123–302, and Carl Schmitt, *Théorie du Partisan*, trans. Marie-Louise Steinhauser (Paris: Flammarion, 1992), p. 208.
7. Pramod K. Nayar (ed.), *The Trial of Bahadur Shah Zafar* (Hyderabad: Orient Longman, 2007), pp. 163–4.
8. Syud Ahmed Khan, *An Essay on the Causes of the Indian Revolt* (Agra: Mofussilite Press, 1859), p. 185.
9. For the former comparison see Mirza Asadullah Khan Ghalib, *Dastanbuy*, trans. Khwaja Ahmad Faruqi (New Delhi: Asia Publishing House, 1970), p. 29; and for the latter Salim al-Din Quraishi (ed.), *Cry for Freedom: Proclamations of Muslim Revolutionaries of 1857* (Lahore: Sang-e-Meel Publications, 1997), p. 41.
10. Khan, p. 129.
11. Leela Sarup (ed.), *The Trial of Mangal Pandey: State Papers* (New Delhi: Niyogi Books, 2007), p. 3.
12. Ibid., p. 12.
13. Ibid., pp. 4, 5, 18.
14. Ibid., pp. 161, 164, 166, 167, 170.
15. Nayar, p. 84.
16. Quraishi, pp. 31–2.
17. Ibid.
18. Nayar, p. 81.
19. Mahmood Farooqui (ed.), *Besieged: Voices From Delhi 1857* (New Delhi: Penguin Viking, 2010), p. 380, square brackets mine.
20. Ibid., p. 102.
21. Quraishi, p. 13.
22. Khan, p. 123.
23. Vishnu Bhatt Godshe Versaiker, *1857: The Real Story of the Great Uprising*, trans. Mrinal Pande (New Delhi: Harper Perennial, 2011), p. 26.
24. Khan, pp. 102–3.
25. Ibid., pp. 178–9.
26. Quraishi, pp. 1–2.

27. Ibid., pp. 34–5.
28. Nayar, pp. 187–8.
29. Ibid., p. 188.
30. Quraishi, p. 22.
31. Sarup, p. 25, square brackets mine.
32. Khan, p. 185.
33. Ibid., p. 129.
34. Nayar, p. 103.
35. Nayar, p. 104.
36. Ibid., p. 70.
37. Ibid.
38. Abdul Latif, *Attharah-sau Sattawan ka Tarikhi Roznamcheh*, ed. Khaliq Ahmad Nizami (Delhi: Nadwat al-Musannifin, 1971), p. 52, translation mine.
39. Nayar, p. 94, parenthesis mine.
40. Ibid., pp. 126–27.
41. Quraishi, p. 102.
42. Ibid., pp. 68–72.
43. Nayar, p. 187.
44. Farooqui, p. 360.
45. For the Mongol idea of a universal empire, one that was inherited by Tamerlane and his Mughal successors, see Eric Voegelin, "The Order of God", in *Anamnesis: On the Theory of History and Politics* (Columbia and London: Univ. of Missouri Press, 2002), pp. 224–79.
46. Nayar, pp. 180–81.
47. Ibid., p. 116.
48. Farooqui, p. 265.
49. Ibid., pp. 365–66.
50. Nayar, p. 186.
51. I am grateful to Dipesh Chakrabarty for bringing this event to my notice.
52. For the importance of "tradition" in the Raj, see Bernard S. Cohn, "Representing Authority in Victorian India", in Eric Hobsbawm and Terence Ranger (eds), *The Invention of Tradition* (Cambridge: Cambridge University Press, 1992), pp. 165–209.

2. A NATION MISPLACED

1. Nathuram Godse, *Why I Assassinated Mahatma Gandhi* (New Delhi: Surya Bharti Prakashan, 1998), pp. 42–3.

2. For a remarkable interpretation of the relationship between Gandhi and Godse see Ashis Nandy, "Final encounter: the politics of the assassination of Gandhi", *At the Edge of Psychology: Essays in Politics and Culture* (New Delhi: Oxford University Press, 1991), pp. 70–98.
3. My interest in the imperial and international character of Indian nationality was prompted and developed over the course of many conversations with the late Carol Breckenridge, for whose ideas and insights on this subject I'm very grateful.
4. M.K. Gandhi, *Satyagraha in South Africa*, trans. Valji Govindji Desai (Ahmedabad: Navajivan Publishing House, 1928) p. 48.
5. See for this Nalini Natarajan, "Atlantic Gandhi, Caribbean Gandhian", *Economic and Political Weekly*, vol. 44 no. 18, 2 May 2009, pp. 43–52.
6. Gandhi, *Satyagraha*, p. 40.
7. Ibid., p. 28.
8. Ibid., p. 208.
9. See for example M. K. Gandhi, *An Autobiography, or the Story of my Experiments with Truth*, trans. Mahadev Desai (Ahmedabad: Navajivan Trust, 2009), pp. 89–90.
10. M. K. Gandhi, "Hindu-Mahomedan Unity", *Young India*, 25 February 1920, pp. 2–3.
11. Ibid., p. 3.
12. For Gandhi's politics of the body, see Joseph S. Alter, *Gandhi's Body: Sex, Diet and the Politics of Nationalism* (Philadelphia: University of Pennsylvania Press, 2000).
13. Gandhi, *Satyagraha*, p. 145.
14. Ibid., pp. 18–19.
15. For nationalism's convoluted rhetoric of numbers see Arjun Appadurai's *Fear of Small Numbers: An Essay on the Geography of Anger* (Durham: Duke University Press, 2006).
16. M. K. Gandhi, *Hind Swaraj and Other Writings*, ed. Anthony J. Parel (Cambridge: Cambridge University Press, 2003), pp. 48–9.
17. Such definitions are scattered across the whole of Vinayak Damodar Savarkar's, *Hindutva: Who is a Hindu?* (Bombay: Veer Savarkar Prakashan, 1966).
18. M. K. Gandhi, *Hind Swaraj*, pp. 51–7.
19. Ibid., p. 49.
20. Gandhi, *Satyagraha*, p. 79.

21. M. K. Gandhi, "Hindu-Muslim Tension: Its Cause and Cure", *Young India*, 29 May 1924, p. 4.
22. Ibid., p. 5.
23. Godse, *Why I Assassinated Mahatma Gandhi*, p. 26.
24. Gandhi, *Satyagraha*, p. 60.
25. Liaquat Ali Khan, *Jinnah-Gandhi Talks* (Delhi: Central Office, All India Muslim League, 1944), p. 16.
26. Ibid., p. 19.

3. IN PRAISE OF PREJUDICE

1. Hannah Arendt, "On Humanity in Dark Times: Thoughts About Lessing", in *Men in Dark Times*, trans. Clara and Richard Winston (San Diego: Harcourt, 1983), pp. 3–31.
2. For a discussion of the gendered implications of a language of brotherhood, see Carole Pateman's *The Sexual Contract* (Stanford: Stanford University Press, 1988).
3. For the classic statement on this contradiction see Carl Schmitt's *The Crisis of Parliamentary Democracy*, trans. Ellen Kennedy (Cambridge: M.I.T. Press, 1992).
4. Karl Marx discusses such depoliticization in his "Critique of Hegel's Doctrine of State", in *Early Writings*, trans. Rodney Livingstone and Gregor Denton (London: Penguin, 1992). p. 20.
5. See Ajay Skaria, "Gandhi's Politics: Liberalism and the Question of the Ashram", *The South Atlantic Quarterly*, vol. 101, no. 4, Fall 2002, pp. 955–86.
6. That Gandhi's call for non-cooperation was carried in Congress only with the help of Muslims who had joined the party in force and packed its sittings is made clear in M. Naeem Qureshi, *Pan-Islam in British India: The Politics of the Khilafat Movement, 1918–1924* (Karachi: Oxford University Press, 2009).
7. M. K. Gandhi, "Mr. Candler's Open Letter", *Young India*, 26 May 1920, p. 3.
8. See, for instance, Kris. K. Manjapra, "The illusions of encounter: Muslim 'minds' and Hindu revolutionaries in First World War Germany and after", *Journal of Global History*, vol. 1, 2006, pp. 363–82, and Harald Fischer-Tiné, "Indian Nationalism and the 'world force': transnational and diasporic dimensions of the Indian freedom movement on

the eve of the First World War", *Journal of Global History*, vol. 12, 2007, pp. 325–44.
9. M. K. Gandhi, "The Khilafat", *Young India*, 28 January 1920, p. 3.
10. Ibid.
11. See for this Uday Singh Mehta, *Liberalism and Empire: A Study in Nineteenth-Century British Liberal Thought* (Chicago: University of Chicago Press, 1999).
12. M. K. Gandhi, "The Turkish Question", *Young India*, 29 June 1921, p. 1.
13. M. K. Gandhi, "Mr. Gandhi's Appeal", *Young India*, 30 June 1920, p. 8.
14. M. K. Gandhi, "The Khilafat", *Young India*, 23 March 1921, pp. 2–3.
15. M. K. Gandhi, "The Question of Questions", *Young India*, 10 March 1920, p. 4.
16. M. K. Gandhi, "Mr. Gandhi's Letter", *Young India*, 10 December 1919, p. 4.
17. C. Rajagopalachari, "Introduction", in *Freedom's Battle, Being a Comprehensive Collection of Writings and Speeches on the Present Situation* (Madras: Ganesh and Co., 1922), p. 6.
18. M. K. Gandhi, "The Question of Questions", *Young India*, 10 March 1920, p. 4.
19. M. K. Gandhi, "The Meaning of the Khilafat", *Young India*, 8 September 1921, p. 3.
20. M. K. Gandhi, "At the Call of the Country", *Young India*, 21 July 1920, p. 3.
21. M. K. Gandhi, "The Khilafat", *Young India*, 23 March 1921, p. 2.
22. M. K. Gandhi, "The Meaning of the Khilafat", *Young India*, 8 September 1921, p. 4.
23. M. K. Gandhi, "Pledges Broken", *Young India*, 19 May 1920, p. 5.
24. C. Rajagopalachari, "Introduction", in *Freedom's Battle*, p. 5.
25. M. K. Gandhi, "The Question of Questions", *Young India*, 10 March 1920, p. 4.
26. M. K. Gandhi, "Khilafat: Further Questions Answered", *Young India*, 2 June 1920, p. 2.
27. M. K. Gandhi, "How to Work Non-co-operation", *Young India*, 5 May 1920, p. 4.
28. M. K. Gandhi, "Mr. Gandhi's Message", *Young India*, 11 February 1920, p. 1, emphasis in original.

29. M. K. Gandhi, "The Question of Questions", *Young India*, 10 March 1920, p. 4.
30. M. K. Gandhi, "Mr. Gandhi's Letter", *Young India*, 10 December 1919, p. 4.
31. M. K. Gandhi, "How to Work Non-co-operation", *Young India*, 5 May 1920, p. 4.
32. M. K. Gandhi, "Khilafat: Further Questions Answered", *Young India*, 2 June 1920, p. 2.
33. M. K. Gandhi, "The Turkish Question", *Young India*, 29 June 1921, p. 1.
34. M. K. Gandhi, "The Mahomedan Decision", *Young India*, 9 June 1920, p. 3.
35. M. K. Gandhi, "Why I Have Joined the Khilafat Movement", *Young India*, 28 April 1920, pp. 3–4.
36. M. K. Gandhi, "Khilafat: Further Questions Answered", *Young India*, 2 June 1920, pp. 2–3.
37. Søren Kierkegaard, *Fear and Trembling*, trans. Alastair Hanway (Harmondsworth: Penguin, 1985), p. 89.
38. Ibid., p. 97.
39. Ibid., p. 106.
40. The best account of this event and its afterlife is Shahid Amin's *Event, Metaphor, Memory: Chauri Chaura 1922–1992* (New Delhi: Oxford University Press, 1996).
41. M. K. Gandhi, "The Non-Co-operation Committee", *Young India*, 23 June 1920, p. 3.
42. Ibid.
43. Ibid., pp. 2–3.
44. M. K. Gandhi, "Pledges Broken", *Young India*, 19 May 1920, p. 5.
45. M. K. Gandhi, "How to Work Non-co-operation", *Young India*, 5 May 1920, p. 4.
46. M. K. Gandhi, "Khilafat: Further Questions Answered", *Young India*, 2 June 1920, p. 3.
47. M. K. Gandhi, "The Non-Co-operation Committee", *Young India*, 23 June 1920, p. 3.
48. M. K. Gandhi, "The Question of Questions", *Young India*, 10 March 1920, p. 5.
49. The classic account here is B.R. Ambedkar's *What Congress and Gandhi Have Done to the Untouchables* (Bombay: Thacker and Co., 1946).

50. M. K. Gandhi, "Letter to R. B. Gregg", 11 November 1947, in *The Collected Works of Mahatma Gandhi* (New Delhi: Publications Divisions Government of India, 1984), vol. XC, pp. 3–4.
51. M. K. Gandhi, "How to Work Non-co-operation", *Young India*, 5 May 1920, p. 4.

4. BROTHERS IN ARMS

1. Gandhi's frequent demands for immediate self-rule did not, however, imply his approbation of haste, for as we shall see he did not value actions by their consequences. On the contrary, Gandhi was not only willing to wait and suffer, but valued slowness for its own sake. See Uday S. Mehta, "Patience, inwardness, and self-knowledge in Gandhi's *Hind Swaraj*", *Public Culture*, vol. 23, no. 2, Spring 2011, pp. 417–29.
2. M.K. Gandhi, *Satyagraha in South Africa* (Stanford: Academic Reprints, 1954), pp. xiv-xv.
3. I am indebted to Richard Sorabji for his comments on an earlier draft of this chapter, which have allowed me to elaborate on Gandhi's view of the future.
4. Mohammad Iqbal, "Presidential address delivered at the annual session of the All-India Muslim Conference at Lahore on the 21st of March 1932", in Shamloo (ed.), *Speeches and Statements of Iqbal* (Lahore: Al-Manar Academy, 1948), p. 53.
5. M.K. Gandhi, *The Bhagvadgita* (New Delhi: Orient Paperbacks, 1980), p. 284. First, third and fourth parentheses mine. While *bhogabhumi* might more literally be translated as a site of enjoyment, the fact that *bhoga* is a kind of passive or receptive enjoyment, as well as the fact that it is counterposed here with *karmabhumi* as a site of action, seems to me to justify its translation as a site of passivity.
6. *Bhagvadgita*, p. 11, parenthesis mine.
7. *Bhagvadgita*, p. 16, emphasis in the original.
8. *Bhagvadgita*, p. 36.
9. *Bhagvadgita*, p. 292.
10. *Bhagvadgita*, pp. 40–1
11. *Bhagvadgita*, p. 183.
12. For a discussion of the way in which the *Gita* became a key text for Indian politics in modern times, see the forum of essays on "The Bhagavad-Gita and Modern Indian Thought", Shruti Kapila and

Faisal Devji (eds), in *Modern Intellectual History*, vol. 7, no. 2, August 2010, pp. 269–457.
13. *Bhagvadgita*, p. 9.
14. *Bhagvadgita*, p. 15, parenthesis mine.
15. *Bhagvadgita*, p. 280.
16. *Bhagvadgita*, p. 260.
17. *Bhagvadgita*, p. 17.
18. *Bhagvadgita*, p. 283.
19. *Bhagvadgita*, p. 283.
20. *Bhagvadgita*, p. 287.
21. For Gandhi's views on conscience, see Richard Sorabji, *Gandhi and the Stoics: Modern Experiments on Ancient Values* (Oxford: Oxford University Press, 2012), chapter 8.
22. *Bhagvadgita*, p. 20.
23. *Bhagvadgita*, p. 155, parenthesis mine.
24. *Bhagvadgita*, p. 84, parenthesis mine.
25. *Bhagvadgita*, p. 59.
26. *Bhagvadgita*, p. 133.
27. *Bhagvadgita*, p. 148.
28. *Bhagvadgita*, p. 49, parentheses mine.
29. *Bhagvadgita*, p. 49, parentheses mine.
30. *Bhagvadgita*, p. 301.
31. For the individuality of this duty, see Sorabji, *Gandhi and the Stoics*, chapter 6.
32. *Bhagvadgita*, p. 157.
33. *Bhagvadgita*, p. 25.
34. *Bhagvadgita*, p. 25.
35. *Bhagvadgita*, p. 14.
36. Nirmal Kumar Bose, *My Days with Gandhi* (New Delhi: Orient Longman, 1974), p. 236.

5. HITLER'S CONVERSION

1. For this see Dorothy Figuera, *Aryans, Jews, Brahmins* (Albany: State University of New York Press, 2002).
2. See, for example, Gerwin Strobl, *The Germanic Isle: Nazi Perceptions of Britain* (Cambridge: Cambridge University Press, 2000).
3. See, for instance, Markus Daechsel, "Scientism and its discontents: The

Indo-Muslim 'Fascism' of Inayatullah Khan al-Mashriqi", in *Modern Intellectual History*, vol. 3, no. 3, 2006, pp. 443–72.
4. Cited in Jyotirmaya Sharma, *Hindutva: Exploring the Idea of Hindu Nationalism* (New Delhi: Penguin Viking, 2003), p. 170.
5. See Subhas Chandra Bose, *The Indian Struggle, 1920–1942* (Bombay: Asia Publishing House, 1964).
6. Mohammad Iqbal, *Thoughts and Reflections of Iqbal* (ed.) Syed Abdul Vahid (Lahore: Sh. Muhammad Ashraf, 1992), pp. 373–74.
7. See for example Jawaharlal Nehru, *The Discovery of India* (New Delhi: Oxford University Press, 1999), chapter 9.
8. Ibid., p. 417.
9. Muhammad Iqbal, "Mussolini", in *Kulliyat-e Iqbal Urdu* (Aligarh: Educational Book House, 1990), pp. 150–51.
10. For this incident and others in which the fascists in Italy and Germany tried cultivating Indian nationalists, see Nehru, *Discovery*, pp. 18–19 and 46–7.
11. Jamil-ud-Din Ahmad (ed.), *Some Recent Speeches and Writings of Mr. Jinnah* (Lahore: Sh. Muhammad Ashraf, 1942), p. 134.
12. Reginald Coupland, *The Indian Problem: Report on the Constitutional Problem in India* (New York: Oxford University Press, 1944).
13. Patrick Lacey, *Fascist India* (London: Nicholson and Watson, 1946).
14. Nehru, p. 388.
15. See Hannah Arendt, "On Violence", in *Crises of the Republic* (San Diego: Harvest Books, 1972), pp. 105–33.
16. M. K. Gandhi, "Statement to the press", *Harijan*, 9 September 1939, in *The Collected Works of Mahatma Gandhi* (hereafter *CWMG*), (New Delhi: Publications Division Government of India, 1977), vol. LXX, p. 162.
17. M. K. Gandhi, "To every Briton", *Harijan*, 6 July 1940, in *CWMG* (1978), vol. LXXII, pp. 229–30.
18. M. K. Gandhi, "What to do?" *Harijan*, 15 April 1939, in *CWMG* (1977), vol. LXIX, p. 122.
19. M. K. Gandhi, "Letter to Adolf Hitler", in *CWMG* (1978), vol. LXXIII, pp. 253–55.
20. See Anthony J. Parel (ed.), M. K. Gandhi, *Hind Swaraj and Other Writings*, (Cambridge: Cambridge University Press, 2003), p. 57.
21. This correspondence can be found in E. S. Reddy, "Gandhi, the Jews and Palestine" (http://www.gandhiserve.org/information/writings_online/articles/gandhi_jews_palestine.html).

22. M. K. Gandhi, "Why not Great Powers", *Harijan*, 12 November 1938, in *CWMG* (1977), vol. LXVIII, p. 94.
23. M. K. Gandhi, "Hindu-Muslim Tension: Its Cause and Cure", *Young India*, 29 May 1924, p. 4.
24. See M. K. Gandhi, "If I were a Czech", *Harijan*, 15 October 1938, in *CWMG* (1976), vol. LXVII, pp. 404–05.
25. M. K. Gandhi, "The Jews", *Harijan*, 26 November 1938, in *CWMG* (1977), vol. LXVIII, p. 138.
26. M. K. Gandhi, "The Jews", *Harijan*, 26 November 1938, in *CWMG* (1977), vol. LXVIII, pp. 138–39.
27. Ibid., p. 241.
28. For an account of Gandhi's views on Palestine, see Simone Painter-Buck, *Gandhi and the Middle East: Jews, Arabs and Imperial Interests* (London: I.B. Tauris, 2008).
29. M. K. Gandhi, "The Jews", *Harijan*, 26 November 1938, in *CWMG* (1977), vol. LXVIII, p. 140.
30. M. K. Gandhi, "Reply to German critics", *Harijan*, 17 December 1938, in *CWMG* (1977), vol. LXVIII, p. 189.
31. M. K. Gandhi, "Some questions answered", *Harijan*, 17 December 1938, in *CWMG* (1977), vol. LXVIII, p. 192.
32. M. K. Gandhi, "Is non-violence ineffective?" *Harijan*, 7 January 1939, in *CWMG* (1977), vol. LXVIII, p. 278.
33. This doctrine, discussed in the previous chapter, receives perhaps its most elaborate exposition in the Mahatma's 1926 commentary on a Sanskrit text. See M.K. Gandhi, *The Bhagvadgita* (New Delhi: Orient Paperbacks, 1994).
34. M. K. Gandhi, "The Jews", *Harijan*, 26 November 1938, in *CWMG* (1977), vol. LXVIII, pp. 139–40.
35. M. K. Gandhi, "Is non-violence ineffective?" *Harijan*, 7 January 1939, in *CWMG* (1977), vol. LXVIII, pp. 277–78.
36. M. K. Gandhi, "The Jewish question", *Harijan*, 27 May 1939, in *CWMG* (1977), vol. LXIX, p. 290.
37. See Hannah Arendt, "The political organization of the Jewish people", in Jerome Kohn and Ron H. Feldman (eds), *The Jewish Writings* (New York: Schocken Books, 2007), pp. 199–201.
38. M. K. Gandhi, "Nazism in its Nakedness", *Harijan*, 18 August 1940, in *CWMG* (1978), vol. LXXII, p. 361.
39. For a discussion of this problem see Hannah Arendt, "Europe and the

Atom Bomb" in Jerome Kohn (ed.), *Essays in Understanding: 1930–1954* (New York: Harcourt Brace and Co., 1994), pp. 418–22.
40. See for instance Gandhi's interview with Margaret Bourke-White, in *Interview With India* (London: The Travel Book Club, 1951), p. 185.
41. M. K. Gandhi, "Talk with an English journalist", *Harijan*, 29 September 1946, in *CWMG* (1982), vol. LXXXV, p. 371.

6. LEAVING INDIA TO ANARCHY

1. M. K. Gandhi, "Hindu University Speech", in *Speeches and Writings of Mahatma Gandhi* (Madras: G. A. Natesan and Co., 1922), pp. 255–56.
2. Penderel Moon (ed.), Archibald Percival Wavell, *Wavell: The Viceroy's Journal*, (London: Oxford University Press, 1973), p. 33.
3. M. K. Gandhi, "A plea for reason" *Harijan*, 2 August 1942, in *The Collected Works of Mahatma Gandhi* (hereafter *CWMG*), (New Delhi: Publications Division, Ministry of Information and Broadcasting, Government of India, 1979), vol. LXXVI, p. 331, emphasis in original.
4. M. K. Gandhi, "Interview to journalist" *Harijan*, 2 August 1942, in *CWMG* (1979), vol. LXXVI, p. 329, emphasis in original.
5. M. K. Gandhi, "Pertinent questions", *Harijan*, 19 July 1942, in *CWMG* (1979), vol. LXXVI, p. 291.
6. M. K. Gandhi, "Interview to the press", *Harijan*, 19 July 1942, in *CWMG* (1979), vol. LXXVI, pp. 295–96.
7. M. K. Gandhi, "A plea for reason", *Harijan*, 8 August 1942, in *CWMG* (1979), vol. LXXVI, p. 331.
8. See for instance M. K. Gandhi, "Letter to Lord Mountbatten, New Delhi, June 27/28, 1947", *CWMG* (1983), vol. LXXXVIII, pp. 225–27.
9. M. K. Gandhi, "To Muslim correspondents", *Harijan*, 12 July 1942, in *CWMG* (1979), vol. LXXVI, p. 277.
10. M. K. Gandhi, "Interview to a journalist", *Harijan*, 2 August 1942, in *CWMG* (1979), vol. LXXVI, p. 329.
11. Quoted in Mahadev Desai, "The Inner Meaning of the Fast", *Young India*, 23 October 1924, p. 9.
12. M. K. Gandhi, "Letter to Lord Mountbatten, on the train to Patna, May 8, 1947", *CWMG* (1983), vol. LXXXVII, p. 435.
13. Ibid., pp. 435–36.

14. M. K. Gandhi, "Interview to Reuter", *Harijan*, 18 May 1947, in *CWMG* (1983), vol. LXXXVII, p. 416.
15. Nirmal Kumar Bose, *My Days With Gandhi* (New Delhi: Orient Longman, 1991), p. 246.
16. Malcolm Lyall Darling, *At Freedom's Door* (Karachi: Oxford University Press, 2011), pp. 35–6.
17. M. K. Gandhi, "Speech at prayer meeting, New Delhi, June 4, 1947", *CWMG* (1983), vol. LXXXVIII, p. 75.
18. M. K. Gandhi, "Discussion with visitors, New Delhi, July 17, 1947", *CWMG* (1983), vol. LXXXVIII, p. 356.
19. M. K. Gandhi, "Speech at A.I.C.C. meeting, New Delhi, June 14, 1947", *CWMG* (1983), vol. LXXXVIII, p. 154.
20. Ibid., pp. 155–56.
21. M. K. Gandhi, "Speech at prayer meeting, New Delhi, July 7, 1947", *CWMG* (1983), vol. LXXXVIII, pp. 296–97.
22. M. K. Gandhi, "Speech at prayer meeting, New Delhi, November 4, 1947", *CWMG* (1983), vol. LXXXIX, pp. 471–72.
23. See, for instance, the speeches gathered in S. M. Burke (ed.), *Jinnah: Speeches and Statements, 1947–8* (Karachi: Oxford University Press, 2000), especially pp. 53, 59, 61, 63, 70, 72, 75, 92, 102, 232.
24. Ibid., pp. 22, 28.
25. M. K. Gandhi, "Speech at prayer meeting, New Delhi, November 5, 1947", *CWMG*, vol. LXXXIX (1983), p. 479.
26. M. K. Gandhi, "Speech at prayer meeting, New Delhi, December 31, 1947", *CWMG* (1984), vol. XC, pp. 334–35.
27. M. K. Gandhi, "Speech at prayer meeting, New Delhi, November 4, 1947", *CWMG* (1983), vol. LXXXIX, p. 473.
28. For examples of Churchill's views on Gandhi, see Penderel Moon (ed.), Archibald Percival Wavell, *Wavell: The Viceroy's Journal* (London: Oxford University Press, 1973), pp. 22–3, 72, 78, 82, 85, 89.
29. M. K. Gandhi, "Speech at prayer meeting, New Delhi, September 26, 1947", *CWMG* (1983), vol. LXXXIX, p. 246.
30. M.K. Gandhi, "Speech at prayer meeting, New Delhi, November 5, 1947", *CWMG* (1983), vol. LXXXIX, p. 480.
31. Ibid.
32. Ibid.
33. Ibid., pp. 480–81.
34. Ibid., pp. 481–82.

35. M. K. Gandhi, "Speech at prayer meeting, New Delhi, October 29, 1947", *CWMG* (1983), vol. LXXXIX, p. 434.
36. M. K. Gandhi, "Speech at prayer meeting, New Delhi, December 29, 1947", *CWMG* (1984), vol. XC, p. 319.
37. See for this Anthony J. Parel (ed.), M. K. Gandhi, *Hind Swaraj and Other Writings* (Cambridge: Cambridge University Press, 2003), pp. 58–65.
38. M.K. Gandhi, "Speech at prayer meeting, New Delhi, January 4, 1948", *CWMG* (1984), vol. XC, p. 357.
39. See, for example, Jamil-ud-Din Ahmad (ed.), *Some Recent Speeches and Writings of Mr. Jinnah* (Lahore: Muhammad Ashraf, 1942), pp. 57, 84, 134, 141, 165, 166, 205, 212, 215.

CONCLUSION

1. M. K. Gandhi, "Interview to Capt. Strunk", *Harijan*, 3 July 1937, in *The Collected Works of Mahatma Gandhi* (hereafter *CWMG*), (New Delhi: Publications Division Government of India, 1976), vol. LXV, p. 361.
2. In a brilliantly provocative essay, Shruti Kapila has argued that truth rather than nonviolence was key to Gandhi's politics. And this meant that not only life, but morality itself had to be subordinated to the imperative of truth as the only absolute value. See Shruti Kapila, "Gandhi before Mahatma: The foundations of political truth", *Public Culture*, vol. 23, no. 2, Spring 2011, pp. 431–48.
3. M. K. Gandhi, "Death—courageous or cowardly", *Harijan*, 30 November 1947, in *CWMG* (1984), vol. XC, pp. 87–8.
4. Nirmal Kumar Bose, *My Days with Gandhi* (New Delhi: Orient Longman, 1999), p. 43.
5. Ibid., p. 66.
6. Ibid., pp. 87–8.
7. For Gandhi's conception of duty and criticism of rights, see Richard Sorabji, *Gandhi and the Stoics: Modern Experiments with Ancient Values* (Oxford: Oxford University Press, 2012), chapter 6.
8. M. K. Gandhi, "Letter to Julian Huxley, May 25, 1947", in *CWMG* (1994), vol. XCV (supplementary vol. 5), p. 142.
9. I am grateful to Ramin Jahanbegloo for this insight into Gandhi's idea of duty.

INDEX

Abbas, Shah: Safavid Emperor, 36
Abdullah, Sheikh: 177, 179–80
Abraham: willingness to sacrifice Isaac, 86
Adharma (non-duty) 105
Afghanistan: 24, 90
Afghans: 37; ethnic identity of, 34
Afridis 179
Alam II, Shah: descendants of, 38
All-India Muslim Conference (1932): speech of Mohammad Iqbal at, 95
Arendt, Hannah: writings of, 67, 126
Arnold, Sir Edwin: translation of *Bhagavad Gita*, 105
Arjuna: depiction in *Bhagavad Gita*, 96–8, 107–8, 114, 116
Ashvinikumars 105
Asian Regional Conference: members attending, 180
Atman (soul) 109, 112
Attlee, Clement: British Prime Minister, 1; writings of, 1
Aurangzeb: anti-Hindu policies of, 22
Australia: dominion status of, 46
Azad Hind Fauj (Free India Army) 179

Bengal: 4, 187; communist government of, 122; killing of Hindus in, 173; province of, 171
Bhishma: depiction in *Bhagavad-Gita*, 99
Bhogabhumi (site of passivity) 98
Bihar 167, 173
Boer Republic 47
Bonaparte, Napoleon: 74
Bose, Nrimal Kumar: 117–18, 188; former secretary of Mohandas Gandhi (1946–7), 117
Bose, Subhas Chandra: military actions against British forces, 122; military forces commanded by, 179–80
Brahmachari (celibate): 54, 112
Brahmacharya (celibacy): 98
British Empire: 29, 44, 73, 75, 160, 177; dissolution of, 1; dominions of, 2, 46, 79, 167; impact of Indian Mutiny (1857) on, 39; official territoriality of, 79
Brotherhood: 91; aspect of hatred, 70–1; Gandhi's views on, 68–71, 89–90, 92; relationship with nationalism, 71
Buber, Martin: 133
Buddhism: 10; influence of, 9

INDEX

Campbell-Bannerman, Sir Henry: 56
Canada: dominion status of, 2, 46
Capitalism: 122
Catholicism: 107
China: 180
Christianity: 21, 38, 58, 76, 129; Bible, 82, 106, 137; conversion to, 14, 20; missionary activity in, 12; nonconformist, 9; presence in India, 52; struggle with Islam, 80–1
Churchill, Winston: 179; British Prime Minister, 127; criticisms of Mohandas Gandhi, 174–5; opposition to Indian Independence, 1, 155
Cold War: 119, 187; Mutually Assured Destruction, 148–9
Colonialism: 12, 15, 25, 120; British, 121; friendship in, 71; interpretation of *Bhagavad Gita*, 104; opposition to, 80; views of pan-Islamism, 78
Communism: 75, 80, 122–3; presence in Bengal, 122; 'scientific' logic of, 5
Concert of Europe: collapse of, 81
Coolies: 51
Coupland, Reginald: 125
Czechoslovakia: 133; political resistance against Nazism in, 129

Darling, Sir Malcolm: visit to India (1946–7), 164
Dayal, Har: experimentation with pan-Islamism, 75
Desai, Mahadev 106
Dharma (duty) 21, 99, 106, 108
Dharma-yuddha (holy war) 94
Dharna: 10
Drona: depiction in *Bhagavad Gita*, 99

Duryodhana: depiction in *Bhagavad Gita*, 99
Dwarkadas, Kanji: 3, 7; criticisms of Jawaharlal Nehru, 1–2; criticisms of Vallabhbhai Patel, 1–2; view of Mohandas Gandhi, 1–2

East India Company: 24; military forces of, 12, 14

Farz (duty) 21
Fascism: 123–5, 136, 143; appropriation in India, 119–20; condemnation of, 123; focus on anti-Semitism, 133; Gandhi's views on combating, 128–30, 140–1; linking with imperialism, 123, 130; Muslim forms of, 121; 'scientific' logic of, 5
First Anglo-Boer War (1880–1): 47
First World War (1914–18): 13, 28, 47, 68, 72, 124, 133; belligerents of, 122; Treaty of Versailles (1919), 78, 81
Forster, E.M.: *A Passage to India* (1924), 70
France: 24, 136; Revolution (1789–99), 13
Franco, Francisco: supporters of, 185

Gandhi, Mohandas Karamchand: 1–3, 5, 8–9, 28, 33, 62, 68–9, 81, 85, 89–90, 97, 113, 115, 141, 154–5, 165–6, 172, 184, 187, 191; *ahimsa*, 10, 143; assassination of (1948), 12, 41, 48, 60, 117, 167; career as lawyer, 9–10; criticism of Zionism, 137–8; education of, 9; family of, 9; fasting of, 39, 116–17; *Harijan* articles, 130, 135, 139; *Hind Swaraj*

INDEX

(1909), 7, 57, 60, 63, 79; interest in Judaism, 133–4, 136, 140, 149; interpretation of *Bhagavad Gita*, 99–107, 109–11, 114, 116, 118, 145, 181; letters written to Adolf Hitler by, 130–2; meeting with Benito Mussolini (1931), 124; meeting with Roland von Strunk (1937), 185; non-cooperative methods of, 2–6, 11, 18, 40, 86; refusal to become four-*anna* member of Indian National Congress (1940), 87; *satyagraha*, 19; *Satyagraha in South Africa* (1922), 44, 49, 94; speeches of, 6, 79, 152, 168, 178; talks with Mohammad Ali Jinnah (1944), 64, 160; view of imperialism, 23, 57–8; Tolstoy Farm, 53–4; view of liberalism, 46–7; view of nationality, 41, 52–3, 56, 64–5; view of nonviolence, 98, 100, 127, 147, 149–50, 163, 170, 174, 189–90; views on brotherhood, 68–71, 89–90, 92; views on combating fascism/Nazism, 128–30, 140–1, 147, 176, 186; *Young India*, 75

Germany: 8, 136; Bombing of Dresden (1945), 188

Godse, Nathuram: 50, 59–61, 64; assassination of Mohandas Gandhi (1948), 48, 60; support for concept of kinship-based communities, 51; view of Gandhi's concept of nationality, 41–3

Gokhale, Gopal Krishna: political mentor of Mohandas Gandhi, 10

Greenberg, Hayim: writings of, 143–4

Harischandra, Raja: 39, 114

Hindu Mahasabha: 126; members of, 121

Hinduism: 12, 14, 16, 21, 25–7, 29, 33, 59, 68, 71, 73, 76, 82, 84, 120, 126, 166; *Bhagavad Gita*, 10, 21, 96–7, 99–107, 109–11, 114–16, 118, 145, 181; *brahmin*, 17, 25–6, 120; *dalit* (Untouchable), 51, 72, 133; *dharna*, 10, 21; gods of, 1, 96–7; influence of, 9; nationalist, 2, 57, 121; presence in Khilafat Movement, 89, 92; *seva*, 72

Hitler, Adolf: 4, 74, 124, 127–9, 179; admiration of, 121–2; banning of duels with pistols, 187; letters written to by Mohandas Gandhi, 130–2; *Mein Kampf*, 119

House of Timur: constitutional neutrality of, 34–5

Houses of Parliament 127

Huxley, Julian: first Director of UNESCO, 190

Imperialism: 57, 63, 79, 95, 124, 126, 162; British, 131; Gandhi's view of, 23, 57–8; linking with fascism, 123, 130

India: 3–4, 9, 38, 42, 55, 69, 73, 80, 160, 166–7, 181–2, 184; Amritsar, 88; Barrackpore, 16; Berhampore, 16; Bihar, 173; Bombay, 10; Calcutta, 17, 19, 117, 122, 164, 188; Chauri-Chaura, 86, 93–4; Christian community of, 52; conversion to, 22; Cawnpore, 12, 19; Delhi, 12, 14, 16, 24, 28–9, 31–2, 36, 168, 173–4, 180; dispute with Pakistan over Kashmir, 176; Government of, 46, 136–7, 179; Guja-

INDEX

rat, 10, 55–6; Hindu population of, 38, 41, 43, 53, 60–1, 72, 117, 134, 153, 158, 160, 168–70, 174, 176; Hyderabad, 176; Independence of (1947), 1, 11; Jallianwala Bagh massacre (1919), 78; Lucknow, 12; Mumbai, 119; Muslim population of, 29, 34, 38, 41, 43, 48, 52–3, 56, 60, 72, 81, 117, 134, 153, 158, 160, 168–71, 173; nationalism in, 11, 14, 33, 51, 57, 72–3, 125; Noakhali, 173–4, 188; Oudh, 24; Partition of (1947), 116, 175, 183, 188; religious traditions of, 112; Round Table Conferences (1930–2), 124; Saharanpur, 59; Sikh community of, 168–71, 174

Indian Mutiny (1857); 11–12, 15–16, 20, 28, 40; brutality of, 13; colonial accounts of, 13; mutineer families, 30; impact on British Empire, 39; impact on religious conversions in India, 22, 25; religious targets in, 14, 17–18, 27, 29; Queen's Proclamation (1858), 39

Indian National Congress: 28, 42, 45–6, 72, 124, 151, 159, 161–4, 167, 179; condemnation of fascism by, 123; electoral performance of (1937), 124; High Command, 125; leaders of, 1, 49, 123; members of, 87; nonviolent practices of, 163; Working Committee, 165–6

Indo-Pakistani War (1947): outbreak of, 177

Indra 105

Inquisition: torturing of victims by, 129

Insaf (justice) 164

Iqbal, Mohammad: 124; All-India Radio broadcast (1938), 123; condemnation of fascism by, 123, 130; speech to All-India Muslim Conference (1932), 95

Iran: 38

Iraq; 124; Baghdad, 34

Islam: 12, 14, 21, 25, 27–8, 34, 51, 59–60, 68, 71, 72, 74, 76, 78, 80, 82, 84, 87, 120, 126; conversion to, 22; dietary practices of, 83; fascist forms of, 121; nationalist, 2, 138–9; presence in Khilafat Movement, 89, 92; Qur'an, 23, 28, 106; sacred sites of, 74; *shaykh*, 26; Shi'ism, 24; struggle with Christianity, 80–1; Sunni, 24, 28

Italy: Rome, 124

Japan: 122, 154, 179; atomic bombing of Hiroshima and Nagasaki (1945), 148, 150, 188; victory in Russo-Japanese War (1904–5), 122

Jainism: 10; influence of, 9

Jesus Christ: 142–3

Jewish Frontier: 143, 146

Jinnah, Mohammad Ali: 65, 125, 166, 171–2; founder of Pakistan, 2, 124; President of Muslim League, 64, 124; speech at Muslim University (1940), 125; talks with Mohandas Gandhi (1944), 64, 160

Jones, Sir William: observations on origins of north Indian languages, 120

Judaism: 8, 58, 77–8, 120; Gandhi's interest in, 133–4, 136, 140, 149; nationalist, 138–9; persecution under Nazi Germany, 59, 121, 125, 132–3, 135, 146, 185

INDEX

Karna: depiction in *Bhagavad Gita*, 99
Kashmir: 177, 180; Hindu community of, 177; Indian-Pakistani dispute over, 176, 178, 182; Muslim community of, 181; Sikh community of, 181
Khan, Ahsanullah: 35, 39; royal physician, 24, 33
Khan, Hulagu: military campaigns of, 34
Khan, Sayyid Ahmad: 26; writings of, 15, 22
Karma (action) 102
Karmabhumi (site of activity) 98
Khilafat Movement: 29, 40, 51, 59, 73, 83, 88; collapse of (1922), 72, 86, 92; failure of, 30; ideology of, 48, 75, 82, 88; impact of, 78–9; members of, 89, 92
Kierkegaad, Søren: *Fear and Trembling*, 85–6
Kipling, Rudyard: *The Ballad of East and West* (1889), 71
Krishna 96
Krishnavarma, Shyamji: experimentation with pan-Islamism, 75
Kruger, President Paul (of South Africa)136
Kurukshetra 107, 116

Landsdowne Lord: 47
League of Nations: 134; efforts following collapse of Concert of Europe, 81
Lenin, Vladimir: 4
Lessing, Gotthold Ephraim: 67
Liberalism: 85, 90, 122; as interest, 77; colonial context of, 69; economic, 60; Gandhi's view of, 46–7; universality of, 76
Linlithgow, Lord (Victor Hope): Viceroy of India, 152

Lloyd George, David: British Prime Minister, 74, 83; foreign policy of, 74, 83

Magnes, Judah: 133
Mahabharata 105
Mao Zedong: 4
Marathas: 37; ethnic identity of, 34
Marx, Karl: view of Indian Mutiny, 13; writings of, 12–13
Mitrata (friendship) 72
Morley, Lord John: Secretary of State for India, 47
Mountbatten of Burma, Lord Louis: agreement with Indian National Congress' Working Committee, 165; role in Partition of India (1947), 165; Viceroy of India, 161–2, 167
Mughal Empire: 14, 28, 31
Mughals: adherence to Islam, 34; ancestry of, 34–5; ethnic identity of, 34
Muni (saint) 112
Muslim League: 87, 121, 126, 151, 159, 161–2, 164, 167; condemnation of fascism by, 123; led by Mohammad Ali Jinnah, 64, 124; members of, 173
Mussolini, Benito: 129, 179; meeting with Mohandas Gandhi (1931), 124

Napoleonic Wars (1803–15): belligerents of, 122
Natal 45
Nationalism: 15, 25, 49, 57, 68, 75, 91, 95, 123; bourgeois, 93; Hindu, 2, 57, 121; Indian, 11, 14, 33, 51, 57, 72–3, 125; Islamic, 2, 138–9; Jewish, 138–9; Pakistani, 14; relationship with

INDEX

brotherhood, 71; view of pan-Islamism, 78
Nazism: 8, 59, 119–20, 125, 127, 147, 176, 185–6; cult of biological purity, 145; focus on Himalayas, 121; opposition to, 127–9, 132; persecution of Jews, 59, 121, 125, 132–3, 135, 146, 185
Nehru, Jawaharlal: criticisms of, 1–2; *Discovery of India*, 126; leader of Indian National Congress, 1–2, 123; writings of, 123
Nepal: 36
Niemöller, Pastor Martin: 142
Non-alignment: 80

Ottoman Empire: 28, 77, 84; collapse of, 47, 68, 72, 83, 85; territory of, 73

Pakistan: 2, 160, 166–7, 171, 180–2, 184; dispute with India over Kashmir, 176; Independence of (1947), 116, 175, 183, 188; nationalist, 14
Palestine: 77–8, 137
pan-Islamism: 75, 78, 84; colonialist views regarding, 78; concept of, 74; nationalist views regarding, 78
Paramatman (universal soul) 112
Patel, Vallabhbhai: criticisms of, 1–2; leader of Indian National Congress, 2
Persia: 24, 36; prevalence of Zoroastrianism in, 51
Poland: Warsaw Ghetto Uprising (1943), 144
Prahlad: 114
Pratap, Raja Mahendra: experimentation with pan-Islamism, 75
Protestantism: 107

Punjab: province of, 171

Qadir, Ghulam: 38
Quit India Movement (1942): 95, 153–4, 156, 160; ideology of, 183; launch of, 151

Rajputs: ethnic identity of, 34
Ruskin, John: influence of, 9
Russian Empire: 24; defeat in Russo-Japanese War (1904–5), 122
Russo-Japanese War (1904–5): belligerents of, 122

Sabarmati (river) 98
Samadarshi (one who sees things equally) 113
Sardar of Kot 164
Satyagraha Ashram 97
Sati (widow-burning): 17
Saudi Arabia: Mecca, 38
Savarkar, Vinayak Damodar: *Hindutuva*, 57; implication in assassination of Mohandas Gandhi, 12
Second World War (1939–45): 2, 119–20, 151, 155, 186; atomic bombing of Hiroshima and Nagasaki (1945), 148, 150; Battle of Stalingrad (1942–3), 188; belligerents of, 135–6, 156–7; Bombing of Dresden (1945), 188; Holocaust, 132
Selborne, Lord (Roundell Cecil Palmer): 47
Seva (service) 72
Shah, Bahadur: 32–5, 37; ancestry of, 38; constitutional authority of, 36–7; mutinous forces led by, 31
Sikhism: 17
Sikhs: 159; ethnic identity of, 34
South Africa: 10, 41, 43, 46, 48, 53,

INDEX

55, 57, 62; Boer population of, 45, 47, 50–1, 55–6, 61; dominion status of, 79; Indian emigrant community of, 41–2, 44, 50, 56, 136, 141–2; Johannesburg, 10, 55, 58; Jewish community of, 58; Muslim community of, 54; Natal, 45; Sindhi community of, 50
Soviet Union (USSR): 80, 122; Stalingrad, 188
Spain: Civil War (1936–9), 185; *Reconquista*, 15
Statesman, The 142
Stead, Mr. (William Thomas) 56
Sthitaprajna (one who is morally constant) 112
von Strunk, Roland: death of (1937), 186–7; meeting with Mohandas Gandhi (1937), 185
swadeshi: origins of, 33
Swadharma (individual duty) 113–4
Switzerland: Geneva, 190
Symonds (Gandhi's South African friend) 58

Thoreau, Henry David: influence of, 9
Tolstoy, Leo: 54; influence of, 9
Transvaal 47
Turkey: 76, 81

United Kingdom (UK): 136, 140, 180; Government of, 30, 36, 76, 147, 158–9, 167; London, 9–10, 105, 124, 127, 142
United Nations (UN): 169, 177, 181–3; Educational, Scientific and Cultural Organization (UNESCO), 190; Human Rights Commission (1947), 190; Universal Declaration of Human Rights (1948), 190
United States of America (USA): 136, 140, 180; African American Civil Rights Movement (1955–68), 59, 133; Civil War (1861–5), 13

Vayu 105
Victoria, Queen: 24, 38; Empress of India, 39
Vivekananda, Swami: significance of, 74

Wallace (figure in Gandhi's commentary on the *Gita*) 107
Wavell, Lord Archibald: Viceroy of India, 152
Westminster Abbey 127

Yajna (ritual sacrifice) 109

Zionism: 77–8; Gandhi's criticism of, 137–8
Zoroastrianism: presence in Persia, 51

213